One of the greatest works of American literature, Mark Twain's *The Adventures of Huckleberry Finn* expresses, through the ruminations of a young, unschooled boy, ironies and inequities in pre–Civil War American society. Huck's journey is both a flight and a quest. He describes the idyllic code of life on a raft: "What you want, above all things, on a raft is for everybody to be satisfied, and feel right and kind toward the others."

THE ILLUSTRATED TIMELINE OF
Western Literature

THE ILLUSTRATED TIMELINE OF
Western Literature

A CRASH COURSE IN WORDS & PICTURES

Carol Strickland, PhD

STERLING

New York / London
www.sterlingpublishing.com
A JOHN BOSWELL ASSOCIATES BOOK

STERLING and the distinctive Sterling logo are registered trademarks of the Sterling Publishing Co., Inc.

Library of Congress Cataloging-in-Publication Data Available

2   4   6   8   10   9   7   5   3   1

Published by Sterling Publishing Co., Inc.
387 Park Avenue South, New York, NY 10016
© 2007 by Sterling Publishing, Co., Inc.
Distributed in Canada by Sterling Publishing
c/o Canadian Manda Group, 165 Dufferin Street
Toronto, Ontario, Canada M6K 3H6
Distributed in the United Kingdom by GMC Distribution Services
Castle Place, 166 High Street, Lewes, East Sussex, England BN7 1XU
Distributed in Australia by Capricorn Link (Australia) Pty. Ltd.
P.O. Box 704, Windsor, NSW 2756, Australia

Printed in China.
All rights reserved.

Sterling ISBN-13: 978-1-4027-4860-8
ISBN-10: 1-4027-4860-4

For information about custom editions, special sales, premium and
corporate purchases, please contact Sterling Special Sales
Department at 800-805-5489 or specialsales@sterlingpub.com.

Book design by Barbara Aronica-Buck

Contents

Acknowledgments and Dedications

My thanks to the fine crew that helped produce this book: Barbara Aronica-Buck for her superb design skills, John Boswell and Kathryn Baxter for making it happen, and Melanie Gold for her patient editing and sympathetic tolerance for my raves and rants.

I beg forgiveness from the many gifted writers whose works I've omitted because of space limitations. And I thank the included authors for the pleasure I've had in re-reading their work and apologize for the brevity of my summaries. If this brief overview inspires browsers to plunge into the primary sources, it's fulfilled its purpose.

I thank my immediate family—dedicated readers all—for their input and encouragement. Family life for me, my husband, Sid, and daughters Alison and Eliza was always enlivened and enlightened by our communal activity: reading, reveling in, and discussing books. At various times, we'd all lose ourselves—and find ourselves—in books. Now my two-year-old granddaughter, Lora Love Rini, has discovered the same joy.

So here's to Lora and her baby brother, Ray, our best hope that the printed word will never die, and to their parents, Alison and Joe. And a toast to ardent readers Eliza Strickland and her new husband, Chris Thompson!

Introduction

"Literature," the critic Bernard Berenson wrote, "is the autobiography of humanity." But what a lengthy autobiography! In the 1600s, an English reader had access to a total of two thousand books. In 2007, more than two thousand books are published each week, including ten thousand novels a year. How do you decide what to read?

This survey is a selective guide to the most enduring literature of the Western world, what Matthew Arnold called "the best that is known and thought" preserved between the covers of books.

Literature is as old as the storytelling impulse. It dates back to our forebears sitting around fires in caves recounting—and embellishing—the day's hunt. Myths—the earliest stories preserved—were humanity's first attempts to describe, understand, and influence the workings of the universe. As literature became more complex in classic Greek drama, it aimed higher: to capture truths about human nature. Since human nature is remarkably stable, even ancient literature has much we can learn from today. This book covers five thousand years of the history of the written word in the West, from legends to the most sophisticated and experimental writing of the Information Age.

" 'Tis the good reader that makes the good book," according to Ralph Waldo Emerson, who insists on "creative reading as well as creative writing." To be a good reader requires much more than following a plot. Since great literature suggests more than it states, it involves interpretation. This timeline provides basic information for decoding a writer's message. Presented chronologically, it helps you see prevailing trends, such as Romanticism or Realism, as well as shifts when authors rebel against past masters to strike out in new directions.

By highlighting the most beloved books that continue to be read and revered, this survey points you to the authors most worth knowing. It will help you choose primary sources you want to read yourself, so you can begin a dialogue with these works of power, passion, and genius. My hope is that sparks from the greatest literary minds will kindle and catch fire in your imagination, bursting into a blaze of pleasure and insight.

What makes these works worth reading is that they can teach, move, and delight us today. A book that merits inclusion in the Western canon never loses its relevance, since, as W. H. Auden noted, "A real book is not one that's read, but one that reads us." By stepping into a character's world, we learn about problems all people face in any era. If you actively engage with a great book, it lifts you to a train of thought with transformative power. You simultaneously escape your time and come back to it with increased wisdom.

As Franz Kafka put it, "A book must be the ax for the frozen sea within us."

How to Use This Book

To make the vast span of Western literature intelligible, this book is divided into four major sections, each with an introduction. These preambles discuss the social, cultural, political, and historical forces shaping each era. Since great art is both timely and timeless, knowing the context helps you understand currents—radical and reactionary—to which authors are responding.

Individual works of literature are displayed in the timeline format, in tandem with a brief text entry on the author's contribution or significance. Some entries highlight a masterpiece; others assess traits of the author's work in general. All captions give you an entrée into cracking the code of what nearly four hundred major writers have to say, how they say it, and why we should care.

In addition, entry texts are color-coded to tell you, at a glance, the works' genre: poetry, drama, nonfiction, or fiction. Sidebars throughout the book break out movements deserving more detail.

This browsable presentation provides a visual and verbal point of entry into key works of Western civilization. Whether you're encountering authors for the first time or refreshing your knowledge, it's like having a fast-moving survey unscroll before your eyes.

Color Key

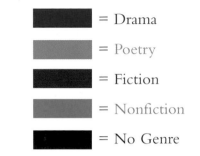

= Drama

= Poetry

= Fiction

= Nonfiction

= No Genre

From Classical to Chivalric: Literature from Antiquity to the Middle Ages

Once nomadic tribes discover agriculture and settle down in the first cities, they turn their attention from subsistence to civilization. Writing develops, first to document trade, then to communicate abstract ideas. The first literature attempts to explain cosmic forces, alleviate insecurity, and appease supernatural forces. This religious impulse creates myth, a universal form of literature that goes back to ancient Mesopotamia and Egypt.

Another primal motive in writing is to praise and memorialize outstanding deeds and individuals, as in the Babylonian *Epic of Gilgamesh*. The earliest legends of rulers and heroes from antiquity reinforce civil order and underline social values. Then there's the human tendency to undermine authority, to follow one's curiosity and ask, "What if . . . ?"—a form of fantasy and satire of ancient lineage.

The earliest literature establishes all these models, still followed today: epic legends, mythological tales, personal testaments, history, philosophy, cautionary stories, and spoofs, rendered in both poetry and prose.

Although the first writing originates in the cradle of civilization along Middle Eastern rivers—the Tigris, Euphrates, and Nile—the true cradle of Western literature is Athens. As the poet Percy Bysshe Shelley says, "We are all Greeks." Homer, writing possibly in the eighth century BC, produces the first indisputable masterpieces, *The Iliad* and *The Odyssey*, stirring epics rooted in our common humanity. Then, around mid-fifth century BC, as the city-state of Athens develops the first democracy, it also produces a flowering of drama, both tragedy and comedy. Performed in amphitheaters and attended by the masses, these plays plumb the heights and depths of human behavior, in language that still resonates today. Athens in the time of Pericles (460–429 BC) is a place of audacious thought and debate. Works from this period—philosophy and history as well as poetry and drama—set the stage for all that is to come.

Alexander the Great spreads the Greek classics throughout his expansive Hellenistic empire, succeeded by the Romans who are equally enamored of Greek thought and literature. Although Rome conquers Greece in 146 BC, Greek literature becomes the template for Latin writers. Until around 500 AD, when the Roman Empire is reduced to its Eastern half, Latin authors expand volubly on Greek models and disseminate them throughout the fifty million people whom Rome rules at its height. Greco-Roman culture becomes the basic lingua franca for Western civilization, from Britain to the Nile and from North Africa to the North Sea.

In 476, when the last Roman emperor is deposed by the Goths, civilization temporarily retreats to the banks of the Bosporus—the city of Constantinople, founded in 330 by Emperor Constantine. There, Greek culture continues to flourish for one thousand years in the Byzantine Empire, preserving the texts of antiquity until their rediscovery in Western Europe during the Renaissance.

St. Jerome laments Rome's fall: "The lamp of the world is extinguished, and it is the whole world which has perished in the ruins of this one city." Yet culture is not totally dim in the Dark Ages. In the former western Roman Empire, after "the Eternal City" crumbles, a new citadel emerges—St. Augustine's *City of God*, a literary icon of the Middle Ages in which Christian faith replaces paganism. In contrast to ancient classical literature, which deals with man, including all his foibles and virtues, valor and vanity, medieval literature, fundamentally religious, deals with man's relation to the deity.

From the sixth century, almost all writing is done by clerics—practically the only literate people—in monasteries. The church attracts the outstanding intellects of the time, and these men and women write primarily theological texts illuminating the Christian faith and the soul's path to salvation. In *scriptoria*, monks copy, illustrate, translate, and preserve ancient texts. More ambitious thinkers like Pierre Abélard and Thomas Aquinas add their own philosophical speculations. During the feudal era, beginning in 900, the Catholic Church is the main force unifying disparate fiefdoms, and monasteries are centers of learning. The Church fills the gap left by the demise of Rome. Christianity, Greco-Roman tradition, and German tribal culture forge a new synthesis.

As barbarians settle Europe and manors ruled by lords arise, folkloric sagas like Norse, German, and Anglo-Saxon legends (first sung by bards in the seventh and eighth centuries) are written down as epic verse. Secular literature and ballads, composed to entertain an audience, gain a foothold, as the first embryonic nations form. From the eleventh to thirteenth centuries, medieval epics, like France's *Chanson de Roland*, celebrate the heroism of knights.

The code of chivalry during these centuries codifies the behavior of nobles, popularized in Arthurian tales of the Knights of the Round Table. Wandering troubadours and poets sing or orate verses, courtly love poems, and popular literature in the oral tradition in vernacular language (as opposed to Latin), a new development.

As commerce increases after the Crusades in the twelfth century, towns grow, along with trade guilds and a middle-class bourgeoisie. Feudalism fades. By the century's end, the first national kingdoms develop in France and Britain. A burgeoning emphasis on education creates universities in Paris and Oxford in the thirteenth century.

For most of the Middle Ages, all Western literature is written in Latin, although oral poems are performed in native, spoken languages; folktales and ballads comprise a rising tide of vernacular literature.

The culmination of the two trends from the beginning of literature through the Middle Ages—writing about both man and God—occurs when Dante Alighieri creates his masterpiece *The Divine Comedy* (1321), fusing classical and Christian thought. Examining politics, society, human life on earth, and the spiritual yearning for the Absolute, this epic poem is vibrant and visionary.

Its counterpart, Geoffrey Chaucer's *Canterbury Tales* (1400), the other high-watermark of medieval literature, is much more down-to-earth. Written in Middle English, the tales run the gamut from low comedy to moralistic fable and are as vivid today as then. From the classical to the medieval period, writers employ their unique voices to explore the complexity of human nature and aspirations, making their words live forever.

The First Writing

In both Egypt and Sumer (Mesopotamia), writing starts as pictures. In Egypt (because it's relatively easy to draw on papyrus), hieroglyphs, or "sacred signs," continue for thousands of years as simplified pictorial symbols. Gradually hieroglyphs evolve from representing objects to ideas and sounds. By 3000 BC specific characters represent vowels and consonants, although still not comprising an alphabet. In Sumer, pictographs (picturelike signs) represent objects, succeeded by ideographs to represent concepts, then signs standing for the sounds of syllables, known as phonetic writing. A scribe produces signs by pressing a reed on soft clay tablets. These wedge-shaped impressions, called cuneiform, spread throughout the Near East until, shortly before the birth of Christ, the Phoenician alphabet replaces them.

3000 BC

4

c. 3000 BC Sumerians in Mesopotamia invent writing in pictograms, which evolves into 600 cuneiform wedge shapes, combined to form words. (Egyptians use simplified hieroglyphs at same time.) Around 500 years later, Sumerians begin to record stories about gods and kings on clay tablets, as seen here.

c. 2300 BC Earliest author known by name, Enheduanna, Assyrian princess (daughter of Sargon), writes verse. Born in kingdom of Ur and high-priestess of moon-god temple, she writes 1st known book of poetry in Western history. Shown here, figure from capital city Uruk.

c. 2000 BC Oldest recorded myth, Babylonian *Epic of Gilgamesh*, inscribed on 11 clay tablets excavated from ruins of Nineveh; tells story of literature's 1st hero. Statue from Sargon II's palace shows Gilgamesh taming lion. In epic, Gilgamesh, who was real king of Uruk in 2700, seeks secret of immortality. During quest, he hears tale similar to Old Testament story of great flood. In both, builder of ark collects family and animals, lands on mountain peak, sends birds to discover if waters have receded.

1500–1100 BC More than 1,000 Sanskrit hymns containing revelations from the gods 1st preserved in oral tradition in India, then collected in Rig-Veda, the oldest major work in an Indo-European language. Rig-Veda contains childlike riddles and deep religious speculations. By c. 600–300 BC, Indian sages collect teachings on theology in Upanishads; 18th-century illuminated page shows Sanskrit manuscript.

c. 1400–1000 BC Hebrew lawgiver Moses, shown as portrayed by Michelangelo, credited with writing the earliest books of the Old Testament: Genesis, Exodus, Leviticus ("Thou shalt love thy neighbor as thyself"), Numbers, and Deuteronomy, also known as the Torah.

1500 BC

c. 1580 BC Egyptians use simplified form of hiero-glyphs to record myths and letters. *Book of the Dead* combines illustrations (here, Osiris) and hieroglyphics, is guide for souls of dead through underworld.

c. 1300 BC Canaanites produce an epic poem on cuneiform tablets, *The Poem of Baal*, about ancient god of rain and fertility and his challenges to other gods. Poem records primitive myths shared by Greeks and other Mediterranean peoples, such as fluctuating periods of growth and dormancy, and death and resurrection of god Baal, shown here as gilded bronze idol.

c. 1000 BC Bible blossoms into polished literature, as an unknown author writes superb book of Job, David composes Psalms, and Solomon is believed to author Ecclesiastes ("To every thing there is a season, and a time to every purpose under the heaven"), Song of Solomon, and Proverbs. In tale of trials and sufferings of Job (portrayed here by José de Ribera), a just man is tested and rewarded: "I am escaped with the skin of my teeth. . . . The price of wisdom is above rubies."

c. 700 BC Farmer-poet Hesiod introduces major Greek gods in epic *Theogony*. His *Works and Days* typifies his didactic streak, introduces concept of lost Golden Age when an eternal springtime of peace and harmony prevailed. "Observe due measure, for right timing is in all things the most important factor." Painting of Pandora based on Hesiod story illustrates downside of unchecked curiosity. Pandora unleashes all the world's ills when she opens forbidden urn. In legend, last spirit to fly out was Hope or, in another version, only Hope remained in the vessel.

c. mid-9th century BC Homer produces 1st undisputed master-piece of literature: *The Iliad*, recounting last days of Trojan War. Portrays humanity and nobil-ity of Achilles, stung by an insult, who chooses glorious death rather than life devoid of honor. Homer's sequel, *The Odyssey*,

narrates the wanderings of Ulysses on his way home. Gripping tale and canny use of flashbacks increase drama. Epics compiled from folktales sung by generations of bards: "From his tongue flowed speech sweeter than honey." Homer creates individualized characters and moving scenes for maximum impact. Mosaic shows Ulysses and his son Telemachus, who together free Ulysses' wife from her suitors to reunite the family. *Iliad* and *Odyssey* are models for all Western epic poems.

Vice may be had in abundance without trouble; the way is smooth and her dwelling place is near. But before virtue the gods have set toil.
—Hesiod

668 BC Assyrian king Ashurbanipal born. He collects royal library of 25,000 clay tablets. Bas-relief from his palace shows king on chariot after victory. Most important literature of Near East, excavated in ruins of his capital Nineveh, preserved thanks to bibliophile king.

6

c. 600 BC Sappho writes simple, intense *Lyrics* on Greek island of Lesbos. Of her 9 books of lyrical poems and hymns, only fragments survive. An early feminist, she chastises women for lack of education. Most famous female poet of ancient world, whom Plato called "the tenth Muse," is possibly portrayed in Pompeii fresco. Legend has it Sappho, after the beautiful but haughty youth Phaon rejected her, hung up her harp and flung herself from a cliff into the sea.

From Epic to Esoteric

Homer's *Iliad* tells the stirring tale of Greeks and Trojans clashing in battle "on the ringing plains of windy Troy," showing the gods' influence on man's fate. His *Odyssey* recounts Odysseus' adventures as he struggles to return from Troy, also the stuff of great heroic legend. Gradually a more personal style of poetry, sung to an accompanying lyre, develops. These passionate poems deal with individual delights and sorrows, rather than national events, as in Sappho's intense evocation of love at 1st sight, "Without Warning":

As a whirlwind
Swoops on an oak
Love stalks my heart.

600 BC

c. 590 BC Legendary Greek writer Aesop, a former slave, delights audiences with *Aesop's Fables*, moralistic folktales based on exploits of talking animals. Story of the hare and the tortoise's race illustrates human vices like hare's arrogance, and virtues such as tortoise's perseverance. "Slow and steady wins the race."

c. 560 BC Although Arion of Corinth performed choral lyrics called dithyrambs around 600, which Aristotle considers root of Greek tragedy, the 1st rudimentary stage play is performed in this year when Greek poet Thespis of Attica presents spoken, rather than sung, dialogue on stage. Thespis is regarded as 1st actor (hence, the word "thespian") and playwright; invents drama by giving chorus members solo lines. Pioneers ludicrous tales in verse to amuse audience and use of linen mask to depict facial expression, shown in image of Greek actor holding mask. In 534, Thespis wins prize at 1st Great Dionysia, theatrical competition held in Athens, precursor to Broadway's Tony Awards.

c. 511 BC Phrynichus, actor and author who 1st uses masks to represent female characters on stage, gains 1st prize for tragedy. Famous for choreography, he improves dances of chorus and transforms light, Bacchanalian plots into serious stories of heroic deeds. His tragedy on the recent capture of Miletus by the Persians is so moving, the audience bursts into wailing. Phrynicus is fined 1,000 drachmas for inflicting pain on viewers. Chorus remains a major player in Greek drama until Aeschylus and Sophocles develop dialogue and action as principal means to convey story.

c. 445–425 BC Herodotus's history of the Persian invasion of Greece establishes him as Father of History. Writing vividly to memorialize "great and wonderful deeds," he's 1st to treat the past rationally and analytically rather than as myth, although he includes tall tales and references to the gods. In story of Persian wars, he provides fascinating digressions into history of Egypt and Babylon. Combines charm with accuracy. "In peace, children inter their parents; war violates the order of nature and causes parents to inter their children."

500 BC

498 BC Greek poet Pindar, shown sculpted in marble, praises winner of footrace in verse. Writes triumphal odes (45 extant) to celebrate military and athletic victories, sung in homecoming parade for winner. Famous throughout Greece for strong rhythm of verse, elevated diction, and bold imagery. Alexander the Great spares Pindar's family home in Thebes when he sacks the city, due to his respect for Pindar's lush lines. "Words have a longer life than deeds."

472 BC Aeschylus's earliest surviving tragedy, *The Persians*, dramatizes Greek victory at Salamis, battle in which he participated. He conjures dramatic conflict by adding another actor (the antagonist), in dialogue with protagonist and chorus. Introduces costumes, props, and scenery. Known for grand language and grandiose subjects, this scene from *The Eumenides* encompasses the struggle between tradition and modernity, the gods and man. With his love of pageantry, startling imagery, and tense, exciting lines, Aeschylus conjures up a chorus of Furies so hideous that women in the audience miscarry and children have seizures, convulsed by terror.

Legend has it that Aeschylus's death in 456 was caused by an eagle, which—mistaking his bald head for a rock—dropped a tortoise from a great height to break its shell. An oracle had prophesied he'd die by a blow from heaven.

c. 441 BC Sophocles, greatest Greek dramatist, writes tragedy of *Antigone*, exploring conflicting claims of public authority and personal morality. Ordered by King Creon to leave her brother's body unburied, Antigone obeys the gods' decrees to honor the dead. Creon sentences her to die for her defiance, bringing manifold tragedy to his family as a result of his pride. When Sophocles is 90, his son drags him to court, claiming the old man is too senile to manage his holdings. In rebuttal, Sophocles recites from the play he is then writing, *Oedipus at Colonus* (illustrated in painting of Oedipus and Antigone): "One word / Frees us of all the weight and pain of life: / That word is love." Verdict: his mental powers are still supreme.

424 BC First truly objective historian, Thucydides, is exiled for poor military performance. During his travels, he observes war between Sparta and Athens, which he documents in *History of the Peloponnesian War,* the 1st history to describe events as fought by human beings rather than manipulated by pagan gods. Focuses on cause and effect, observable fact as described by eyewitnesses. His aim: "an exact knowledge of the past as an aid to the interpretation of the future." Includes high-flung speeches by major characters, such as Pericles's funeral oration: "But the bravest are surely those who have the clearest vision of what is before them, glory and danger alike, and yet notwithstanding go out to meet it."

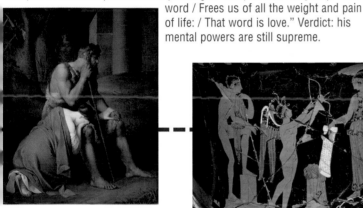

431 BC Euripedes writes *Medea* and other Greek tragedies like *Electra* and *Phaedra,* employing keen psychological insight, social criticism, and characters with human, even homely, traits. In contrast to Aeschylus and Sophocles, he undermines accepted concepts like the inferior position of women and glorification of war. This vase painting shows the title character of Medea, smitten by love for Jason. Even though a queen, Medea is all too human when, rejected by Jason, she wreaks awful, heartbreaking vengeance by killing their children. "The gods visit the sins of the fathers upon the children."

The Greek Miracle

Literary creativity explodes in Periclean Athens (c. 461–406 BC), along with philosophy, science, art, architecture, and the development of democracy. Authors produce the 1st written history and the 1st lyric poetry. Playwrights invent both tragedy and comedy, showing man contesting divine and secular authority before succumbing to destiny. Open-air plays are attended by the masses and reinforce the ideals of reason, harmony, and moderation. Techniques of suspense, characterization, poetic dialogue, and meaningful action leading to a climax evolve. As Sophocles sums up: The reverential Aeschylus creates moral tales instinctively, the irreverent Euripides paints people as they really are, and Sophocles portrays them as they ought to be. Athens, where writers scale the heights and depths of humanity, is, Thucydides says, "an education for all Greece."

414 BC Aristophanes pens scathing masterpiece of Greek comedy, *The Birds*, ridiculing the gods, public figures, and the state. A practitioner of farcical Old Comedy with its bawdy songs, obscene jokes, and political lampooning, Aristophanes uses broad humor and burlesque to defang authority. Shows originality in inventing novel situations, characters, and new worlds rather than recycling history. His heroine in *Lysistrata*, shown here, harangues Athenian women not to make love with their husbands until the men cease making war: "There is no animal more invincible than a woman, nor fire either, nor any wildcat so ruthless." Typical play shows protagonist embarking on impossible task, yet characters seem natural even in absurd circumstances.

c. 350 BC Greek philosopher Aristotle writes *Poetics* after studying with Plato, seen in detail of Raphael's painting of the two men. In *Poetics*, Aristotle's great contribution to literary theory, he describes poetry as imitation of life, animated by an instinct for harmony and rhythm. Tragedy elicits emotions of fear and pity, which, after reaching a climax, result in a cleansing release or catharsis. The hero falls from a height of eminence due to his tragic flaw—often pride (hubris). This reversal of fortune occasions a revelatory discovery or epiphany.

350 BC

399 BC Socrates, convicted on charge of impiety and corruption of youth, drinks poison hemlock, dies. Before age 40, oracle at Delphi pronounced him the wisest man in Greece, which puzzles Socrates until he realizes that others, unconscious of their ignorance, claim knowledge while he admits his lack of certainty. His philosophy, known through Plato's *Dialogues*,

Aristotle's treatises, and Xenophon's discourses, teaches that virtue starts with self-knowledge, evil comes from ignorance. Socrates invents inductive reasoning, seeking to advance from particulars to universal truths and wisdom. "The unexamined life is not worth living." He lives creed by posing provocative questions to encourage independent thought in his acolytes. Pompeii mosaic shows philosophers debating in *stoa*.

317 BC Greek playwright Menander, shown in mosaic reading before two comic masks, wins 1st prize for witty play *The Grouch*. In more than 100 comedies, he masters New Comedy, which, with its ingenious plots, is more literary and romantic than Old Comedy satires. Refines plays from coarse, indecent farces. Ignoring own advice, "the man who runs may fight again," when Menander loses to rival playwright, he's so mortified, he hurls himself into the sea and drowns at age 51.

c. 300 BC Arabs find most famous library of antiquity in Alexandria, Egypt, center of Hellenistic culture. At its maximum of perhaps 700,000 papyrus scrolls, it is said to contain all the world's knowledge. According to legend, in 642 AD, Caliph Omar is said to order the volumes burned; so numerous were they that the conflagration heated city's baths for 6 months. Modern authorities term story apocryphal.

Some things are easier said than done.
—Plautus

55 BC Cicero's *De Oratore* sets standard for elocution, as in painting of Cicero denouncing Cataline in Roman Senate. Greatest master of Latin prose writes on philosophy, politics, literature, and rhetoric. Is foremost author to make Latin a great literary language, transformed from straightforward prose to language of subtle sophistication, conveying strong emotions and complex ideas. His rhetoric is rolling, colorful, and symphonic, geared to persuade the reader through articulate pyrotechnics. When his enemy Marc Antony gains power, Cicero is declared an outlaw and murdered. Last words before he's decapitated: "There is nothing proper about what you are doing, soldier, but do try to kill me properly." His head and hand are displayed in Forum where Cicero's golden tongue once reigned supreme. Antony's wife plucks out Cicero's tongue and jabs it repeatedly with hairpin. "The shifts of fortune test the reliability of friends."

100 BC

191 BC Roman comedy author Plautus writes *Pseudolus* in Latin, introducing stock character of sly servant. Nicknamed "Flatfoot," Plautus was so impover-

ished in youth he worked in a flour mill (shown in painting), turning the crank for a baker, until he could sell his 1st play. In 40-year career, Plautus develops Latin musicals and broad comedies for crowds who come to see gladiator contests and bear baiting. Later playwrights like Shakespeare, Molière, Ben Jonson borrow from his plots and characters.

AVE ATQVE VALE

54 BC Catullus, 1st successful lyric poet in Latin, dies after penning explicit amoral poems, which celebrate his erotic love ("over head and heels") for mistress Clodia and his boyfriend Juventius. Writes about intensely personal experiences, not for a public audience but for his fellow poets. Visiting his brother's grave near Troy, Catullus composes famous ode ending, *"Frater, ave atque vale"* ("And forever, O my brother, hail and farewell!"), illustrated in ink drawing by Beardsley.

11

51 BC Julius Caesar writes historical narrative *Commentaries on the Gallic War*. *De Bello Gallico* begins: "All of Gaul is divided into three parts," describes victory over Gallic chief Vercingetorix, shown here surrendering to Caesar in 52 BC. Known for brisk, clear prose (on defeating king of Pontus, Caesar famously says, *"Veni, vidi, vici"* ("I came, I saw, I conquered"), Caesar produces accurate, concise history.

19 BC Roman poet Virgil (author of *The Aeneid*, supreme epic poem glorifying Augustus and Rome) dies. Painting shows Virgil reading *The Aeneid* to Emperor Augustus and Octavia. Epic recounts adventures of Aeneas, legendary founder of Latin culture, on journey from Troy to Italy. Bursts with patriotism, nobility, and imperial pride. "As long as rivers shall run down to the sea, or shadows touch the mountain slopes, or stars graze in the vault of heaven, so long shall your honor, your name, your praises endure."

50 BC

c. 50 BC Lucretius kills himself before finishing 6-volume philosophical poem, *On the Nature of Things*, expounding Epicurean philosophy. Argues with eloquence and passion that everything in universe operates according to natural laws, not influenced by supernatural powers. Exhorts readers to seek pleasure in the serenity of philosophy without fear of death. Page from *De Rerum Natura* shows the 4 elements, which scientists consider the essence of all matter.

8 BC Horace, Roman poet of conversational *Odes* that satirize through ridicule, dies. Polished, urbane style illustrates his Aristotelian doctrine of moderation: "It is the mountaintop that the lightning strikes." He advises equanimity and indifference to the vagaries of fate: "Whoever cultivates the golden mean avoids both the poverty of a hovel and the envy of a palace."

4 BC Seneca the Younger, Roman dramatist, born in Spain. Becomes orator at Roman courts where his skill attracts jealousy of Emperor Caligula. Writes 8 surviving tragedies while in exile, like *Medea* and *Oedipus*, based on Greek tragedies. Later becomes Nero's tutor, gains fame and power. Stoic principles tested when Nero commands him to kill himself. ("What fools these mortals be.") Slits wrists and calmly bleeds to death. ("Light griefs are loquacious, but the great are dumb.") Main importance is as link between classic theater and Renaissance rebirth of drama. In translation, his plays influence French and British dramatists, who raise the genre to great heights.

5 AD Tales in Ovid's *Metamorphoses* transmit classical myths to Roman world. Epic treatment of history of world from chaos to its epitome under Julius Caesar focuses on examples of instability in nature. Shows unpredictability of life in series of miraculous transformations, as when Daphne mutates into laurel tree or in painting, shown here, foreshadowing Eurydice's conversion to a pillar of salt after her husband, Orpheus, turns back to look at her. Although a fascinating and elegant storyteller, this cosmopolitan, sophisticated writer is banished to a savage fishing village on the Black Sea where he dies: "Time the devourer of all things."

c. 66 AD Greek Plutarch, after traveling to Rome, writes *Parallel Lives*, 46 biographies of renowned Greeks and Romans showing how character influences destiny. "The mind is not a vessel to be filled but a fire to be kindled." Researches extraordinary figures in Greek and Roman history to discover what traits make men heroic or ignoble. Painting illustrates Plutarch's *Life of Marius*, imprisoned at Minturnae, south of Naples.

> I see the better way, and I approve it, yet I follow the worse.   —Ovid

c. 61 AD Petronius writes racy Latin "novel," *Satyricon*, satire of immorality in Roman Empire. Petronius, hailed as *Arbiter Elegantiae*, advises Nero on licentious lifestyle, takes decadence to new levels of extravagance. *Satyricon* humorously describes outrageous behavior in colloquial prose. As in this painting of torchlight revelry under Nero, Petronius and his cronies sleep all day and carouse all night. Petronius slashes his wrists after Nero arrests him, invites pals to watch his leisurely demise.

100 AD Roman poet Juvenal writes 1st of 16 vitriolic satires, denouncing laxity, tyranny, and debauchery under Emperor Domitian. Diatribes full of pithy epigrams: "Peace visits not the guilty mind." Satire of outrage cynically contrasts corruption of wealthy Romans to traditional Roman virtues. "Count it the greatest sin to prefer life to honor, and for the sake of living to lose what makes life worth having." Invective reaches apex, targets flaws of Roman manners and morals, as in Beardsley's drawing of lustful Messalina returning from baths. Juvenal's banished for mocking a favorite of the emperor, dies in exile.

MESSALINA.

13

397 Roman theologian Augustine, shown in painting by Botticelli, begins classic autobiography *Confessions*, frankly recording his religious development and arguing for unified church doctrine encompassing his views on sin,

predestination, and grace. After barbarian Visigoths sack Rome in 410, St. Augustine writes *City of God*. Book envisions new Christian society rising from ruins of paganism, assures believers that even though "the eternal city" fell, faith endures. Repenting of his wild youth in Carthage, where he fathered an illegitimate child, Augustine explains in *Confessions*, "I loved not yet, yet I loved to love. . . . I sought what I might love, in love with loving."

c. beginning of 6th century
Byzantine poet Musaeus writes poem, *Hero and Leander*, in Greek. Tells of virgin priestess, Hero, in love with youth, Leander, who swims across Hellespont to be with her.

She lights lantern in tower to guide him until one night after she succumbs to his seduction, wind blows out light and Leander loses his way, drowns. Grief-stricken Hero dives into waves to share his watery grave

524 While in prison awaiting trial on trumped-up treason charge, Roman philosopher Boethius writes *The Consolation of Philosophy*, most influential work of Middle Ages. Reflecting on vagaries of fate, he frames debate as dialogue with Lady Philosophy, seen in illustrated manuscript. She explains why the good suffer and evildoers appear to prosper, locating peace not in outward achievements but inner riches. "Why then, O mortal men, do you seek that happiness outside, which lies within yourselves?" Considered last of the Romans, Boethius is last Western writer for seven centuries to translate ancient Greek, attempting to balance faith and reason; transmits Neoplatonism to Europe. "Nothing is miserable but what is thought so, and contrariwise,

every estate is happy if he that bears it be content." Consoling philosophy severely tested when Boethius, tortured by rope tightened around his head until eyes pop out, is clubbed to death.

Be always displeased at what thou art, if thou desirest to attain to what thou art not.   —St. Augustine

670 Caedmon is earliest known English Christian poet. Venerable Bede recounts how uneducated shepherd, inspired by vision, spontaneously declaims religious verse in monastery at Whitby. "Hymn of Creation" is English verse version of Scripture.

14

Golden Age of Medieval Philosophy

Scholasticism, a philosophy that flourishes in the 13th century, derives from Plato via Augustine and Boethius, as elaborated by Abélard and Aquinas. The growth of universities (particularly in Paris and Oxford) in the 1200s and the availability in the West of Latin translations of Aristotle's works is credited with Scholasticism's rise. This philosophical system aims to synthesize Christian doctrine with philosophy derived from Aristotle, linking faith and rational inquiry. Logic and observations of the senses are used to deepen an understanding of religious beliefs and provide a rational underpinning. Dominicans and Franciscans expand universities and pursue philosophical speculations in 2 forms of Scholastic literature: question (posing and defending a thesis against objections) and commentary.

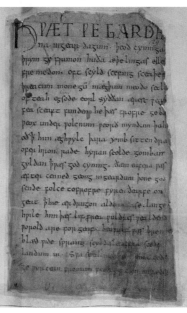

c. early 8th century Oldest English epic, *Beowulf*, derived from oral Scandinavian folktales by anonymous Northumbrian bard. Beowulf fights monster Grendel and Grendel's mother in 1st part. Part II narrates Beowulf's old age, defeating a dragon, and hero's funeral after an honorable life. Merges pagan and Christian elements in alliterative verse. Old English poem sung at festive gatherings, 1st major poem in European vernacular language.

BEDE LE VENERABLE

c. 800 Celtic monks produce *Book of Kells*, Latin gospels with abstract and animal illustrations, intricate lettering, and ornate patterns of illuminations. Probably copied in monastery in County Meath, Ireland, by monks who fled to Kells to escape Viking invasion of Scotland. Pictured, page from Gospel of St. John.

731 The Venerable Bede, a Benedictine monk, finishes *The Ecclesiastical History of the English People* in Latin prose. Scholar of both Greek and Latin writes 40 works of biblical commentary and summaries of knowledge of his day. *Ecclesiastical History* covers history and legends of Britain from Roman invasion by most learned man in western Europe.

c. 900 Famous Arabian tales, *A Thousand and One Nights,* supposedly related by Scheherazade night after night, without revealing the conclusion, in order to postpone her execution. Sultan imagines no woman is virtuous after his wife is unfaithful, resolves to marry new wife every evening and have her strangled at dawn. Despite his vow, Scheherazade marries him, then evades her fate by telling fascinating tale but always breaking off before completing it. After 1,001 nights, Sultan gives heart to her, hailing her as liberator of her sex. Classic tales include Ali Baba, Sinbad the Sailor, Aladdin.

1136 Scholar and theologian Pierre Abélard (1079–1142) recounts his love affair with his brilliant pupil Héloise in *Historia Calamitatum Mearum*. His brilliant career as lecturer at University of Paris terminated by ill-starred romance. The pair secretly marry, but her uncle hires thugs to castrate the scholar. Both Abélard and Héloise seek refuge in church, he to become a monk, and she abbess of a convent. Their exchange of poignant love letters describing their suffering is basis of their fame. Abélard is also known as leading exponent of Aristotelian rationalism applied to church dogma, but his attempt to reconcile faith and reason is considered heresy.

1066 Early version of French ballad *Chanson de Roland* sung before Battle of Hastings to encourage French resistance. Heroic poem creates national myth around Charlemagne's knight Roland and his courage in battle. Roland's 20,000-man army is ambushed in mountain pass by 400,000 Saracens, fights valiantly until only 60 remain alive. Roland blows his

ivory horn to call the main French force, cracking it with the power of his blast and bursting the veins of his neck. Most famous example of medieval *chanson de geste*, which sings of heroic deeds. Page of French text shows young Roland, crowned figure, bishop, and attendants.

1140 An unknown bard records "Poema del Cid," recounting the exploits of Spanish national hero El Cid in combat against the Moors. Characterized as the perfect Christian knight, the 11th-century soldier of fortune appears as a champion in much beloved epic poem.

1200–1216 German epic poem *Parzival* by Wolfram von Eschenbach is famous chivalric tale, source for Wagner's *Parsifal*. Wolfram is wandering Bavarian knight whose lyrical compositions combine humor and spiritual depth. Story of simpleton who overcomes obstacles and temptations to become king of the Holy Grail, based on French folktale by Chrétien de Troyes.

The Cult of Courtly Love

Courtly love is a medieval code of manners that flourishes in France and England, a highly conventional set of principles that elevates a noble lady above her slavishly adoring courtier. Probably derived from the songs of wandering minstrels, the code requires a knight to suffer for his lady love and prove his devotion by noble deeds. In these highly regulated rules of conduct, the lady is beautiful, chaste, and worshipped from afar by her gallant knight. The underlying message is that romantic love and marriage are incompatible, for union with the beloved is unattainable, although she still inspires the courtier to heroic feats. First popularized in southern France around 1100, the code spreads to northern France, England, Germany, and England. Its principles inform the King Arthur story cycles, *Tristan and Iseult*, *Troilus and Cressida*, and the Lancelot legend by Chrétien de Troyes. This convention of the subjective experience of love and intense emotion greatly influences later literature.

c. 1221 Italian poets develop 14-line sonnet form, in which 1st 8 lines (octave) state a proposition, followed by a sestet of 6 lines with the resolution. By 1341, Italian sonneteer Petrarch so esteemed, he is crowned poet laureate with wreath on Capitol Hill in Rome, a ceremony revived from antiquity. An avid scholar of ancient Roman literature, Petrarch invents proto-Renaissance humanism, is perhaps 1st modern man. Dominant theme of poetry is love for flesh-and-blood Laura, which occasions inner conflict—both ecstasy and despair. "To be able to say how much you love is to love but little." First to downgrade medieval virtue of asceticism for new appreciation of earthly joys.

c. 1230 French allegorical *Romance of the Rose* establishes poetry-of-love genre. Courtier attempts to woo lady love in 1st part, illustrated in watercolor by Dante Gabriel Rossetti. Second part, composed in 1275, is more bawdy and satirical. Both very popular for 3 centuries, 1st sung in noble courts by roving troubadours and later preserved in illuminated manuscripts.

17

1248 Islamic Persian poet Rumi writes stories, pours out grief for death of mentor in music, dance, lyric poems. Followers become "whirling dervishes," perform Sufi worship in dance and music. Rumi's epitaph: "When we are dead, seek not our tomb in the earth, but find it in the hearts of men."

1274 St. Thomas of Aquinas, leading Scholastic philosopher, completes *Summa Theologica.* A great unifier, Aquinas's goal is to join reason and faith. Seeks to reconcile Christian theology with Aristotelian rationalism. Dominican monk, often called the Angelic Doctor, summarizes knowledge of God and man, drawing on both theology and philosophy. Nicknamed Dumb Ox as a student because he was deliberate in manner and quite portly, Aquinas rigidly applies reason in voluminous writings, in simple, precise Latin. Aquinas, pictured in painting by Zurbarán, leads medieval quest to "Christianize Aristotle."

1307–1321 On cusp between the demise of Middle Ages and debut of Renaissance, poet Dante Alighieri composes allegorical masterpiece *The Divine Comedy,* inspired by idealized love for Beatrice, seen in manuscript image meeting Dante. In epic poem, Virgil guides poet through hell (*inferno*) and purgatory (*purgatorio*) toward heaven (*paradiso*). Dante's Beatrice (symbolizing divine love and revelation) then conducts him to God. Universal drama of story deals with individual's quest for the Absolute and humanity's struggle for peace. First significant author to write in vernacular Italian and one of finest poets in any language, Dante is revolutionary in using Tuscan Italian rather than Latin and timeless in elaborating universal tale of man's fall and redemption.

1300

1348–53 Italian Giovanni Boccaccio writes witty prose tales in *Decameron.* Framing story refers to 10 youths who flee Florence in year of the plague, 1348. In their refuge in a hilltop villa, they exchange stories over 10 days, such as tale of Griselda, pictured here. Although based on folktales and chivalric legends, Boccaccio injects new secular spirit, satirizing follies of knights and debunking obsolete ideals of feudalism. Bawdy tales suffused with irony and down-to-earth realism rather than moral purpose—a sharp departure from otherworldly tone of medieval literature.

c. 1362 Unrhymed, alliterative poem *Piers Plowman* ascribed to William Langland of Malvern, England. Narrator describes in rustic dialect many allegorical visions on pilgrim's road to salvation. Characters personify entities like Conscience, which persuades people to reject the Seven Deadly Sins. Considered greatest Middle English poem before Chaucer.

1387 Father of English poetry Geoffrey Chaucer launches saucy *Canterbury Tales* in Middle English with prologue: "Whan that Aprill with his shoures soote / The droghte of March hath perced to the roote, / And bathed every veyne in swich licour / Of which vertu engendred is the flour." Leaves masterpiece unfinished at his death in 1400. Story revolves around group of travelers on springtime pilgrimage to a martyr's shrine at Canterbury who tell stories to enliven the journey. Earthy, 5-times-married Wife of Bath (seen in illustration) relates story of knight who must answer crucial question: "What do women most desire?" Ugly hag provides answer (sovereignty) on condition that knight marry her. When he grants her sovereignty, she changes to youthful beauty. Chaucer's innovations include wide range of narrators from every social level, diverse voices reflecting tellers of tales, individualized portraits and dramatic interaction of characters. Ribald humor makes stories a delight.

c. 1375 Middle English develops more sophistication as seen in "Sir Gawain and the Green Knight," vivid verse narrative in tradition of Arthurian romance. Sir Gawain is courageous and courtly, accepts challenge of mysterious Green Knight, even though it means he must be killed himself in 1 year. To fulfill promise, Gawain travels to castle where a beautiful lady tests his integrity. Elegantly constructed narrative makes this a high point of Middle English literature. Here, Sir Gawain presents himself to King Arthur and Guinevere.

Medieval Female Writers

Chaucer's vivacious Wife of Bath says, "By God, if women had written stories . . . they would have written more wickedness of men than all the spawn of Adam may address." Despite the patriarchal system in Europe that limits opportunities for women, several manage significant contributions to literature. Twelfth-century Marie de France, perhaps the 1st woman writer in France, composes passionate, vernacular poems in Old French decrying the lack of respect for women. Others are the learned abbess Héloïse (Abélard's love), the visionary hermit Julian of Norwich, the mystic Margery Kempe, and the scholarly Christine de Pisan, one of the 1st to support herself by writing, who refutes misogyny and the oppression of women in medieval society. Less well known are Dhuoda, an early medieval writer born c. 803, who, after studying works of antiquity and acquiring vast learning, writes in Latin; the German nun Hrotsvitha of Gandersheim (c. 930–990), the 1st known playwright of the Middle Ages; Hildegard of Bingen (1098–1179), a mystic, writer, and composer; the mystic Marie d'Oignies (1167–1213); and abbess Gertrude the Great (1256–1302).

From Renaissance Seed to Baroque Bloom: An Age of Discovery and Recovery

Renaissance means "rebirth" in French. This spirit of revival in learning and Humanism, based on a challenge to religious orthodoxy and a rediscovery of antiquity, characterizes the era after the Middle Ages. With increased secularization and focus on individualism, creativity in the arts explodes. Baldassare Castiglione and Niccolò Machiavelli in Italy, the cradle of the Renaissance, trumpet these new concepts of the importance—and power—of secular man. In Elizabethan England, towering figures like William Shakespeare, Christopher Marlowe, John Donne, and Ben Jonson make this period rival in brilliance the Golden Age of Greece. French writers like François Rabelais, Michel de Montaigne, Pierre Corneille, Jean Racine, and Molière join the parade of genius.

The Renaissance really begins in fourteenth-century Italy, when a new appreciation for classical learning sprouts. Stimulated by emphasis on the value of human life found in ancient texts, scholars call themselves *humanists*. While medieval scholars studied natural history, mathematics, and theology, they'd ignored pagan literature. Now Renaissance writers read history, poetry, prose, and plays from the past. "What does it advantage us to be familiar with the nature of animals," asks Petrarch, the first Italian humanist, "while we are ignorant of the nature of the race of man to which we belong?"

Humanists, in their lofty concept of individual potential, view themselves as equals of past literary giants. A mania for classical manuscripts sweeps Europe, as works by the most important Latin writers surface in monasteries from beneath inches of dust collected over centuries of neglect. From Constantinople, Greek manuscripts flood Italy. As the value placed on learning and living fully in an increasingly secular world expands, so does the estimate of an individual's importance.

By the beginning of the sixteenth century, translators reintroduce classical works and concepts into the mainstream of Western culture. As a result of the cult status of ancient literature, many writers imitate Ciceronian Latin, and the development of vernacular literature—that is, works not written in Latin—lags. Gradually, a renewed emphasis on the freedom and dignity—even nobility—of mankind encourages writers to express their own views, resulting in literature with a more personal voice. Prose becomes more pithy, shedding its oratorical flourishes.

After printing with movable type begins around 1455, the technology rapidly spreads. The price of books drops by seven-eighths, and books become widely available. With a larger audience, literature can appeal to the tastes of ordinary people. Pamphlets and tracts circulate freely, and knowledge and new ideas reach a widening circle, quickening intellectual life and literary ambition.

With the Renaissance ideal of man at center stage, a sophisticated cultural outlook flows northward from Italy, combining with native traditions to produce indigenous literature in France, England, Germany, and Spain. In poetry, foreign forms and classical models merge with native folklore and ballads in vivid, exuberant styles. Many monarchs either import brilliant writers or cultivate local talents to add luster and high-level entertainment to their courts.

In the sixteenth century, northern humanists (in contrast to Italians, who are stuck on classical models) immerse themselves in exposing social ills (often through satire) and proposing reforms. Desiderius Erasmus and Sir Thomas More in England, François Rabelais and Michel Montaigne in France, and Miguel de Cervantes in Spain criticize the stagnant status quo.

The greatest glory of Renaissance literature is the appearance of national, secular drama, which begins in Italy in the mid-fifteenth century with improvised performances called commedia dell'arte. Theaters increasingly pop up throughout Europe, presenting classical drama catering to aristocratic tastes in France and Italy and national themes appealing to the masses in England and Spain. Since this embryonic art form lacks strict conventions, writers freely experiment. Shakespeare changes plays from narrative to fully dramatic.

The growing emphasis on the individual and his place in the physical world generates concern for contemporary challenges facing a world in flux. Sweeping changes unsettle society, economics, politics, and the collective mentality. The sixteenth century, marked by the Reformation, brings religious upheaval, civil conflict, and warfare. The Protestant Church develops, then the Counterreformation in the late sixteenth and seventeenth centuries reestablishes the clout of the Catholic Church. Baroque-style mysticism and the intense religious piety of Metaphysical poets like Donne coincide with the Counterreformation. Highly ornamented literature with extravagant wordplay is also characteristic.

From the sixteenth century to the mid-seventeenth, national states with central governments replace feudal units. Sovereign nations compete for power and glory. As trade increases, a middle class arises. Revenues inflate royal coffers, supporting standing armies. With the Church no longer the ultimate arbiter, religious wars and power politics rage in Europe.

It's an age of exploration, as navigators, traders, missionaries, and conquerors fill in the blanks on the world map. Before 1500, Europeans lived on only four million contiguous square miles with minimal trade with Africa and Asia. In the next 150 years, they discover new continents in the western hemisphere. Products and wealth pour into the Old World. Colonies become outposts of European culture and institutions, giving rise to literature shaped by new conditions but reflecting established positions.

In this age of geographic, political, and commercial expansion, mercantile capitalism, financed by joint-stock companies, arises. An economic and social revolution enriches European civilization, while absolute monarchs still hold sway on the European mainland. But by the late seventeenth century, sparks of new liberal ideas begin to circulate, which will burst into the flame of revolution in the eighteenth century.

A new spirit of religious tolerance and independent inquiry grows. After 1600, the first seeds of the Age of Reason, to be known as the Enlightenment when it blossoms in the eighteenth century, take root. Science inexorably advances, capped by Sir Isaac Newton's explanation of gravity in 1687. New worlds revealed by the microscope and telescope have a liberalizing effect, hastening intellectual emancipation. The scientific revolution values natural laws, knowable by the mind, over supernatural forces. This new outlook causes writers to reexamine age-old problems, which are theoretically solvable by reason.

In literature of the seventeenth century, this trend downplays emotion and elevates logic, bringing a renewed reverence for the classical spirit. Especially in France, classical forms are venerated and imitated by playwrights like Corneille, Racine, and the witty Molière.

From the first primitive stirrings of native literature to a pinnacle of perfection and a leveling off of refinement, this period represents a pivotal transition from medieval to modern. Measuring up to the humanists' respect for mankind's potential, these centuries are perhaps the most fertile ever in nurturing masterpieces of literature. As Shakespeare's Miranda exclaims in *The Tempest*:

How many goodly creatures are there here!
How beauteous mankind is!
O brave new world
That has such people in't.

1455 Johannes Gutenberg uses his new invention, a printing press with moveable type, to produce a Bible in Mainz, Germany. Mechanical process enabling mass production of books quickly spreads throughout Europe.

Invention of Printing

Printing fosters the rapid diffusion of knowledge by making accessible rediscovered Greek and Latin texts from antiquity (in their original language and in translation). For the 1st time, learning, the new Humanism, and civilization are spread through the written word rather than through visual images. Literacy increases, encouraging the production of new literature. In Italy, scholars write mainly in Latin and Greek, but in northern Europe more books appear written in the vernacular, which widens their audience and promotes the spread of ideas. The dispersal of humanistic values throughout Europe is largely attributable to printing, as volumes are no longer painstakingly produced by hand. Now books disseminate knowledge and innovations, which flow from the birthplace of the Renaissance in Florence to the rest of Europe.

1455

1456 French poet François Villon, considered best poet of late Middle Ages, writes facetious parody *Le Petit Testament*. His *Grand Testament* of 1461 laments pathos of human life with bitter humor. Barely saved from gallows after brawls, homicide, and miscellaneous unsavory escapades, Villon, a romantic rascal, disappears in 1463. Most famous line: "But where are the snows of yesteryear?"

1467 Ballad about legendary Swiss hero William Tell sung to arouse patriotism. In legend, Tell refuses to pay homage to foreign despot, is ordered to shoot apple off son's head as punishment. Tell succeeds but is jailed. Later shoots tyrant and incites revolt leading to independence.

1474 William Caxton prints 1st book in English (at Bruges, Belgium). In all, he prints about 100 books, some his own translations from French. Uses 8 fonts of type and adds woodcut illustrations c. 1480. As 1st printer in England (1476), he superbly crafts books, which become staples of literature of the time: Boethius, Geoffrey Chaucer, and John Gower, along with chivalric legends. Ad from 1477 offers printed book "good chepe."

Jf it plese ony man spirituel or temporel to bye ony pyes of two and thre comemoracios of salisburi vse enpryntid after the forme of this prelet lettre whiche ben wel and truly correct, late hym come to welmonelter in to the almonelrye at the reed pale and he shal haue them good chepe ·:·

Supplico stet cedula

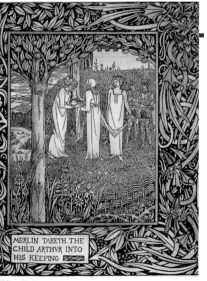

MERLIN TAKETH THE CHILD ARTHVR INTO HIS KEEPING

1485 Sir Thomas Malory's *Le Morte d'Arthur* printed by Caxton. Malory writes 8 prose romances while in prison, serving time for robbery, extortion, and murder, finishes in 1470. Caxton's title is inaccurate, for tales recount picturesque adventures of "King Arthur and His Noble Knights of the Round Table." Dramatic narrative, colorful accounts of tournaments, and simple, rhythmic language make it standout of late medieval literature.

1502 Gil Vicente, playwright known as "the Portuguese Plautus," performs *Monológo del Vaquero* (*The Herdsman's Monologue*) for queen just before she gives birth. Writes many popular comedies denouncing society's vices. Brings Italian humanism to royal courts in plays ranging from farce to comedy to tragicomedy, inhabited by vibrant characters. Whether bitingly satirical or devout, his works are suppressed during the Inquisition because they expose corrupt clergy and court pomposity. Contrasts poverty of masses to glory and wealth of Empire. Shown, king and queen in 1st illustrated book printed in Portugal.

1500

1509 Dutch scholar Desiderius Erasmus, seen in portrait by Hans Holbein, writes satire *In Praise of Folly*. Influential essay by this great humanist chastises abuses and corruption of Roman Catholic Church and folly of pedantry. He personifies folly, abetted by ignorance and drunkenness, who consorts with pals like self-love, laziness, and flattery. Written in 1 week, the book is enormously popular. It questions all authority, and Erasmus becomes the most famous man in Europe for a decade.

1513 Florentine statesman Niccolò Machiavelli authors infamous political treatise, *The Prince*. Includes general philosophy and practical advice on prince's behavior toward his subjects. To maintain power, it is safer for ruler to be feared than loved. Ruthlessness toward foes gets thumbs-up as a necessity, but irrational cruelty is not recommended. Cynicism of later works determines his reputation for intrigue and diabolical malice, but as pioneering political scientist, writing in clear, vigorous style, he is unmatched.

1528 Baldassare Castiglione's *Il Cortegiano* (*The Courtier*) offers Italian aristocrats advice on courtly manners. Framed as series of conversations between nobles, book describes ideal courtier as handsome, aristocratic, courageous, and well versed in arts and letters. Code of conduct and etiquette is influential throughout Europe, gives picture of elegant Renaissance court life. Castiglione, seen in portrait by his friend Raphael, dies in Toledo, Spain, victim of the plague.

1516 Italian epic and lyric poet Ludovico Ariosto publishes 1st edition of *Orlando Furioso*. Expanded, final version published just before his death in 1532. Writer of poems, satires, and plays is best known for long, romantic, narrative poem set among Charlemagne's knights and their adventures against Saracens.

It is not necessary for a prince to have piety, faith, humanity, integrity, and religion, but it is necessary to seem to have them.
—Machiavelli

1532 French comic masterpiece *Gargantua*, followed by *Pantagruel*, by François Rabelais appears. Gargantua is gigantic medieval folk hero, father of immense Pantagruel. He bursts from the womb shouting, "Drink, drink, drink!" and the story increases in buffoonery from there. Satirizes contemporary French society, including antiquated education at Sorbonne, despotism, and oppressive atmosphere of monasteries. (Rabelais is a monk.) In Books III–V, Pantagruel morphs into a Renaissance man questing for knowledge. Burlesque humor of comic genius disguises scrutiny of serious issues. Illustration by Gustave Doré shows Parisian throngs marveling over Gargantua at Notre Dame.

1542 Italian commedia dell'arte begins, establishes stock figures of Pierrot, Columbine, Harlequin, and Pulcinella. Actors perform familiar plots but improvise dialogue. Plays crammed with comic business: sight gags, slapstick, horseplay, and old jokes. Lively, exaggerated, ribald stories involve complex romantic intrigues. Combines music, acrobatics, masks, fools, and farce-like vaudeville—hung on bare outline of plot. Shown, Harlequin and the clown Zanni perform.

Harlequin. Zany Cornetto.

Renaissance in France

The Renaissance arrives with a bang in the 16th century, producing great achievements like the boisterous fun of Rabelais, the gentle sensuality of Pierre de Ronsard, and the magnificent common sense of Montaigne. In the 17th century, Classicism reigns supreme, especially in theater. Playwrights like Corneille, Racine, and Molière write in a polished style, while in poetry and satire Jean de la Fontaine and in prose Blaise Pascal and François de la Rochefoucauld dissect the oddities of human conduct. Traits that are considered consummately French appear: sophisticated wit and imagination and a dazzling show of rational debate.

1550 BC

1547 Marguerite of Navarre's poetry *Marguerites de la Marguerite des Princesses* published. Queen of Navarre is sister of French king Francis I. With her mother, the 2 women negotiate his release from captivity in Spain, treaty known as The Ladies' Peace. Her court is refuge for Calvinist religious reformers. Her religious verse, influenced by humanism and mysticism, is nonorthodox. A collection of 72 short stories, many about the unhappy lot of women, is published after her death in 1549, titled *Heptameron*, her best-known work, modeled on *Decameron*.

1550 Pierre de Ronsard writes *Odes*, France's 1st lyric poetry modeled on Horace and Pindar. In 1552 he publishes graceful love poems in Petrarchan sonnet form. Called "the Prince of Poets," he encourages writing in French, rather than Latin, to establish modern literature but uses classical and Italian forms.

1551 Sir Thomas More's *Utopia* describing ideal society is translated into English from original Latin (1516). Imaginary island of Utopia (name means

"no place" or "good place"), founded on reason, is run according to highest humanist ideals. Inhabitants own no private property, practice tolerance, and their society is without crime, misery, poverty, or injustice. The English humanist scholar and saint defends Roman Catholicism and holds major government positions, rising to Lord Chancellor in 1529. Unwilling to accept Henry VIII as head of English church, More is beheaded. On mounting the scaffold, he quips: "See me safe up: for my coming down, I can shift for myself." Before execution, More proclaims he is "the king's good servant, but God's 1st."

1562 Italian Torquato Tasso writes romantic epic poem *Rinaldo* at age 18. After Tasso begins his masterpiece, *Jerusalem*, epic about Crusades, the Duke of Ferrara sends poet to mental asylum, where he suffers for 7 years. After his release, Pope plans to crown him poet laureate in Rome, but, before ceremony in 1595, Tasso dies. He is later considered

a tragic hero by Lord Byron and Johann Wolfgang von Goethe. *Jerusalem* is finest poem of Counterreformation, with strong religious motif, romantic subplots, and exciting chivalric elements recounted in elevated classical style. Shown, Tasso entertains nobles at ducal court.

1557 *Songes and Sonettes* by Sir Thomas Wyatt published after his death in 1542. Courtier-poet, shown in Hans Holbein's portrait, serves crown as ambassador to Spain. Henry VIII imprisons him twice in Tower of London. (Wyatt's 1st cousin—and possibly his mistress—is ill-fated Queen Anne Boleyn.) His verse introduces Continental innovation (the Petrarchan sonnet) and irregular rhythm to English literature. Lyrics, full of virile energy and robust spirit, berate fickle lovers. Wyatt poignantly recalls past amorous pleasures in "They flee from me, that sometime did me seek, / With naked foot stalking in my chamber."

1563 Thomas Sackville introduces new spirit to Elizabethan literature with "Induction" in *The Mirror for Magistrates*. Statesman who gives up poetry, "his 1st love," at age 25 is pioneer in English literature. "Induction" is considered best poem in what C. S. Lewis calls the "Drab Age" between Chaucer and Edmund Spenser. It describes poet's descent into hell; similar to *Inferno* by Dante Alighieri. In gloomy verse of high literary quality, personifies Death and Revenge with pictorial power. Book intended as cautionary example of rulers

who suffer tragic fates. Reflects new Renaissance concept in which man's own faults, as well as Fortune, determine fate.

1569 Spanish mystic literature blossoms with rhapsodic, spiritual writers like Teresa de Ávila. Saintly nun runs away from home at age 7 to seek martyrdom at hands of Moors. Leads reform of Carmelite community and founds 17 convents. Describes ecstasy and despair of her spiritual life in more than 400 intense letters and autobiography. Uses simple, powerful imagery overflowing with passion, wisdom, humor, and practicality. Revives religious fervor in Counterreformation Spain and beyond.

Elizabethan Theater

During the reign of Queen Elizabeth I (1558–1603), London becomes the scene for a glorious outburst of plays rivaled only by those of Periclean Athens. Despite complaints from church officials that plays lead to public laxity and are often lewd and indecent, they develop rapidly as a form of public entertainment. Many playhouses are built and acting companies spring up to meet the demand for performances. Encouraged by Elizabeth and the nobility, playwrights deal with both serious and light themes. Many stories are drawn from antiquity and English history. Miraculously, in one generation, British dramatic literature ascends from infancy to sublime maturity, creating works without parallel in literature. Clergymen protest that the ungodliness of plays is causing the plague, however, and in 1642 Parliament orders all stage plays suppressed. Playhouses close until the Restoration in 1660.

1572 Greatest Portuguese poet Luís Vaz de Camões publishes seafaring epic *Os Lusíades*, which is compared to Homer and Virgil in scope and ambition. His life fraught with events—he loses eye fighting the Moors as a young man, is jailed several times, serves in India, the Middle East, Africa, and Macao. Shipwrecked in the Mekong, he survives by floating on a plank, saves his manuscript but sees his Chinese lover drown before his eyes. Finally arrives back in Lisbon to publish masterpiece, which tells of Portuguese explorers and links Greek mythology to Christian ideology and demand for heroism. Universality and grandeur of epic glorify Golden Age of Portugal.

1576 Actor James Burbage opens 1st public theater in London, which becomes enormously popular. His son, the actor Richard Burbage, builds famous Globe Theater in 1598 and performs Shakespeare's plays. Globe's exterior is hexagonal with a circular interior and a roof over only the stage. Audience stands in pit or sits in stalls built around walls. Public performances staged in afternoon (admission fee: 1 penny), attended by all social classes, who boisterously express their reactions. Richard Burbage acts all great parts in Shakespeare repertory, is most popular English actor who excels in tragedies like *Richard III*.

1578 John Lyly combines light fantasy and romantic comedy in *Euphues: The Anatomy of Wit*. Educated at Oxford, Lyly brings the prose pastoral to England from Italy. Creates court comedies, which veil flattering allusions to queen and nobility in allegory and classical stories. Popularizes elaborately witty dialogue and gently amusing,

elegant entertainment. His pageant, *Euphues and His England*, gives name to "euphuism," pedantic, superrefined use of language. A contemporary characterizes Lyly, a favorite of the Earl of Essex (pictured): "He is but a little fellow, but he hath one of the best wits in England." Lyly's writing is great hit with sophisticated nobility, ignites rage for polished, artificial style of speech, highly ornamented with rhetorical flourishes.

The Tragicall Historie of the Life and Death of Doctor Faustus.

With new Additions.

Written by C H. M A R.

Printed at London for *John Wright*, and are to be sold at his shop without Newgate. 1631.

1587 Christopher Marlowe captures spirit of the age, defying moral and metrical rules in his drama *Tamburlaine the Great*. Like his tragedy *Dr. Faustus* (1588), play is written in blank verse, with powerful rhythms that Ben Jonson calls "Marlowe's mighty line." *Faustus* is powerful portrayal of ambition, remorse, and despair; arouses terror and pity in audience. Noted for debauchery, Marlowe is stabbed in head in barroom brawl in 1593, dies at age 29. Verse expresses power and glory of youth against inevitable decay of time, as in "The Passionate Shepherd to His Love": "Come live with me and be my love, / And we will all the pleasures prove. . . ."

1575

1580 Michel de Montaigne invents the personal, discursive essay in his sensible *Essais*. Educated by a tutor who speaks only Latin to him until age 6, Montaigne gives up law for writing. In conversational prose, he examines his own experiences to glean moral lessons rooted in common humanity. He strips away dogma, uses concrete imagery and amusing digressions. "Man is quite insane. He wouldn't know how to create a maggot, yet he creates gods by the dozen."

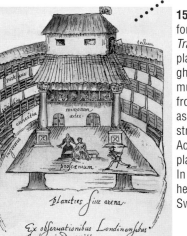

1589 Sir Thomas Kyd ignites vogue for revenge dramas with *The Spanish Tragedy*. Most popular and influential play of the era, tragic drama involves ghosts and nobles in tangled plot of murdered lovers. Stage awash in blood from multiple killings. Not as poetic as Marlowe and Shakespeare, Kyd's strength is his grasp of tragic form. Accused of heresy and atheism, playwright is tortured and imprisoned. In 1594, his spirit broken by disgrace, he dies in poverty at age 36. Pictured, Swan Theatre, London, c. 1596.

1590 Sir Philip Sidney's prose romance, *The Arcadia*, is printed posthumously. Sidney, an ideal Humanist, soldier, gentleman, and poet, combines life of service and action with refinement and dignity. Dies in 1586 after giving his armor to another soldier, is mortally wounded but offers his canteen to dying foot soldier saying, "Thy necessity is greater than mine." *Arcadia* is complicated pastoral tale praising courage and heroic life in consciously artistic style. Poem from *Astrophel and Stella* poses paradox: "When Nature made her chief work, Stella's eyes, / In colour black why wrapt she beams so bright?"

Golden Age of English Poetry

England, after defeating the Spanish Armada in 1588, embarks on a period of stability, prosperity, and expansion that undergirds astonishing achievements in literature. So many poets (Walter Raleigh, Spenser, Marlowe, Robert Herrick, Andrew Marvell, Donne, Jonson, Shakespeare, and John Milton) produce so many masterpieces that this epoch from the late 16th century to the close of the 17th century may never be equalled. The new concept of the nobility of man, embodied in Classical Humanism, and the medieval focus on death and decay merge to produce a sweeping view of life—both heroic and mortal. Two main forms of poetry arise: Cavalier (in the Jonson mode of lively love poems) and Metaphysical (patterned after Donne's complex, intellectually challenging poems).

1600

1590 Edmund Spenser's allegorical poem cycle, *The Faerie Queen*, Books 1–3, published. Considered "the prince of poets in his time," Spenser is learned and dedicated to his art and his country. Writes pastoral poems, sonnets, satire, complaints, and heroic epic with philosophic (Christian-Platonic) content. Called by Milton "our sage and serious poet." Shown, Red Cross Knight, serving the Faerie Queen (symbol of Queen Elizabeth), slays dragon.

1605 First part of book on which his reputation rests, Miguel de Cervantes's *Don Quixote de la Mancha* published. Cervantes fights valiantly in naval Battle of Lepanto, off western Greece, is seized by Barbary pirates, and enslaved in Algiers until ransomed. *Don Quixote* tells of addled country gentleman so deluded by reading chivalric romances, he undertakes mission to save the world. He constantly mistakes ordinary folk for lofty romantic figures, like sheep for armies; regards peasant girl as his ideal lady Dulcinea. Quixote is undaunted, although he encounters one mishap after another, assisted by pragmatic rube Sancho Panza. Book satirizes folly of idealism while creating immortal characters and panoramic view of 17th-century Spain.

William Shakespeare: What a Piece of Work

Hamlet's soliloquy expresses both Shakespeare's faith in man and awareness of his inevitable fall: "What a piece of work is man! How noble in reason! How infinite in faculties! In form and movement how express and admirable! In action how like an angel! In apprehension how like a god! The beauty of the world! The paragon of animals! And yet, to me, what is this quintessence of dust? Man delights not me."

In range, Shakespeare has no peer. His works delve into universal human problems like jealousy (*Othello*), ambition (*Julius Caesar* and *Macbeth*), families (*Hamlet*), and aging (*King Lear*). He composes sublime sonnets from 1593 to 1601, but his 38 plays in blank verse are best known. His characters evince all the qualities of humanity: from cruel, desperate, shallow, and ridiculous, to tender, kind, and profound. They speak in dazzling repartee, using striking turns of phrase and stunning metaphors. His verses throb with music and bristle with ideas. Grounded in our common fallibility, his plays strike chords that echo in the heart. Although Shakespeare's characters suffer for their mistakes, the moment of disaster brings moral cleansing and spiritual triumph. Happiness may not be possible, but a man can do the right thing and gain insight.

1605 *King Lear*, perhaps Shakespeare's greatest tragedy, performed in London. Shakespeare (1564–1616) writes patriotic history plays, then comedies like *Twelfth Night*. In early 1600s, turns to tragedies (pictured, Laurence Olivier as Hamlet). Hamlet called "1st modern man," as philosophical prince struggles with conscience and consequences. Shakespeare considered greatest literary genius of all time for depth and complexity of characters, dialogue rising to peaks of lyric beauty. Plots borrowed from antiquity, with perfect fidelity to human nature, embodied in dramatic action and speech. His friend Ben Jonson pronounces best epitaph: Shakespeare "was not of an age, but for all time."

1606 Ben Jonson satirizes society in colorful play *Volpone* (*The Fox*). Poet laureate, soldier, actor, and writer—a man of enormous learning—Jonson pioneers realistic comedies and satirical humor in plays unlike anything seen before. Creates absurd contemporary characters, lampoons social follies. "Mischiefs feed / Like beasts, till they be fat, and then they bleed" (*Volpone*). In theater, Jonson rivals Shakespeare, and in nondramatic poetry, Donne. Begins as bricklayer, distinguishes self in battle as English champion against single enemy, drifts into theater and into trouble. Kills actor in duel but escapes hanging. In drama, argues for honest realism: "deed and language such as men do use" and employs savage comedy as tool to deflate egos. Most famous verse: "Drink to me only with thine eyes, / And I will pledge with mine; / Or leave a kiss but in the cup / And I'll not look for wine."

Glories, like glow-worms, afar off shine bright,
But look'd too near have neither heat nor light.
—John Webster, *The White Devil*

1613 John Webster's *The Duchess of Malfi* presents horrific view of human nature. Play tells story of Italian duchess who, against her powerful brothers' wishes, marries a commoner whom she loves. The brothers seek vengeance but find doom. Webster, accused by T. S. Eliot of always seeing "the skull beneath the skin," revels in excessive violence as duchess and husband suffer due to cruelty of her insane twin brother, the duke. Dark, macabre works and onstage bloodbath foreshadow Gothic strain of 18th-century literature.

1623 Sir Francis Bacon publishes Part I of his ambitious project *Instauratio Magna* (*Great Renewal*) in Latin, outlining his theory of knowledge. Bacon possesses most brilliant philosophical mind of era, attacks blind acceptance of medieval dogma, which impairs learning. According to Bacon, scholars should study nature rather than accept truisms and should connect theory to reality. Prose is well crafted, clear, and precise. As a contemporary says, "he did rather drive at a masculine and clear expression than at any fineness or affectation of phrases."

1630 John Winthrop becomes governor of Massachusetts Bay colony, creates orderly theocratic society in Boston. Delivers famous sermon on ship bound for New World. Declares that Puritans should serve as "model of Christian charity," an example of right living for all. "For we must consider that we shall be as a city upon a hill, the eyes of all people are upon us." Shown, Winthrop disembarks in 1630.

1624 Captain John Smith publishes *The Generall Historie of Virginia, New England, and the Summer Isles*, account of his leadership of Jamestown colony in 1607–1609. Smith spends his last years in London recounting his expeditions to New World. His books serve as propaganda to lure colonists to new territory. Paints America as land of riches, abundance, and freedom. Shown, illustration of Smith's adventure as captive of local Indians, when 12-year-old Pocahontas pleads with her father, Powhatan, to spare Smith's life.

1633 John Donne's poems, rife with parodox, irony, and wit, published 2 years posthumously. Poetry termed Metaphysical for its complicated conceits, somber passion, and curious turns. Ingenious metaphors fuse thought and emotion in colloquial rhythm. As Anglican priest, Donne, considered the thinking-man's poet, writes immortal sermons, meditations, and holy sonnets. "Death, be not proud, though some have called thee / Mighty and dreadful, for thou art not so; . . / One short sleep past, we wake eternally, / And death shall be o more; death, thou shalt die."

1625

1633 English Metaphysical poet George Herbert finishes *The Temple* in year of his death. Herbert's devotional poems are like love poems to God, intense, vivid, gushing with joy or anguish, delight or despair. In form, poetry is ingeniously structured and artful, with colloquial rhythms and homely imagery. His poems represent, he says, "a picture of the many spiritual conflicts that have passed between God and my soul."

> Dare to be true: nothing can need a lie;
> A fault, which needs it most, grows two thereby.
> —George Herbert, *The Church Porch*

Too Mortal for the Club

The ultraconservative *Académie Française* not only is notorious for resisting innovations in language, it also resists admitting authors of unquestioned literary merit who seem too *outré* or *déclassé* for the aristocratic tastes of its members, who are known as "immortals." Among the outstanding writers conspicuous by their absence are: Molière, Jean-Jacques Rousseau, Honoré de Balzac, Gustave Flaubert, Stendhal, Émile Zola, and Marcel Proust. The 1st woman (Marguerite Yourcenar) is not elected until 1980, 345 years, after the Académie is founded. As criteria for membership, literary achievement is all well and good, but—*évidemment*—loyalty to the state and social presentability count as well.

1635 French literary figures establish *Académie Française* to uphold standards of linguistic usage and vocabulary, credited with maintaining purity of classic French. Membership confined to 40 "immortals," supposedly most distinguished writers (shown, in assembly). Académie issues dictionary and grammar text, which resist evolution of language or admission of new words. (In 1680, Louis XIV founds state theater *Comédie-Française*. Its continuing mission is to preserve classics of French theater to keep heritage alive.)

1635 Spanish playwright Lope de Vega dies at age 72, after prolific career in which he wrote more than 1,800 plays, 450 of which survive. Second only to Cervantes in reputation, Lope invents the 3-act *comedia*, pioneers range and scope of modern drama. As precocious youth, writes 1st play at age 14, is adored by masses who call him "a freak of nature." Works fast without revising; some plays written in only 24 hours. Once composed 15 acts in 15 days (5 comedies in 2 weeks). Specializes in plot-driven, "cloak-and-dagger" dramas about Spanish nobles and their intrigues, like *El Perro del Hortelano* (*The Dog in the Manger*).

1637 At age 31, French dramatist Pierre Corneille writes most famous work, *Le Cid*. In this landmark of dramatic literature—the beginning of modern French drama—Corneille adheres closely to classical unities of time and place as prescribed by Aristotle. Beauty of expression and depth of feeling make

tragedy superior to anything seen before in Paris. Romantic hero struggles between love and honor. Corneille writes 30 plays, both tragedies and comedies, with intricate plots and imaginative verse. Pioneers internal drama of soul in conflict, rather than earlier, action-driven plots. Seen here, set for his 1650 play *Andromède*.

1639 Printing begins in North America in Cambridge, Massachusetts. Rev. Joseph Glover packs printing press on ship bound for Massachusetts Bay Colony, but dies en route. His widow hires Stephen Daye to operate press. In 1640, 1st book in North America printed, *Bay Psalm Book*, "newly turned into metre, for the edification and comfort of the saints." When Glover's widow marries Henry Dunster, president of Harvard College, press becomes forerunner of Harvard University Press.

THE FIRST PRINTING PRESS BROUGHT TO AMERICA.

1640 *El Alcalde de Zalamea* (*The Mayor of Zalamea*) by Pedro Calderón de la Barca, one of Spain's best-known literary figures, is performed. Calderón is court dramatist under Philip IV in Madrid, a model Christian poet and knight devoted to the Spanish Crown. He enters priesthood but continues to write plays in which the Spanish *pundonor*, or point of honor, is carried to an extreme.

1640

1643 Sir Thomas Browne's *Religio Medici* (*A Doctor's Religion*) attempts to discover sustaining faith. Browne—a great literary stylist and significant thinker—is physician who questions religious practice and tenets, dispassionately examines conflict between reason and faith. Assumes benign, detached air resonant with curiosity in writings. Prose style quaintly cadenced and ornate.

1648 Cavalier poet Robert Herrick publishes pastoral and love verses like "To the Virgins, to Make Much of Time." One of most charming lyric poets,

Herrick follows classical models, but his content is rooted in English countryside. Lustily praises youthful passion. "Corinna's Going A-Maying" is wake-up call: "Get up, sweet slug-a-bed and see / The dew bespangling herb and tree." As country cleric, Herrick breaks the mold, keeping a pet pig that he teaches to drink from a tankard, and once, cursing, throws his sermon at drowsy congregation. Title of poem "To live merrily and to trust to good verses" could be his motto.

c. 1650 English Metaphysical poet Andrew Marvell's "To His Coy Mistress" urges lover to "seize the day" because "at my back I always hear / Time's winged chariot hurrying near. . . . The grave's a fine and private place, / But none I think do there embrace." Few poems published before 1681, since Marvell fears to publicize satirical poems in time of political upheaval. Reputation soars in 20th century after T. S. Eliot praises his poems' intellectual subtlety and depth. Works show brilliant wit, eloquence, and lyric grace.

THE
TENTH MUSE
Lately sprung up in AMERICA.
OR
Severall Poems, compiled
with great variety of VVit
and Learning, full of delight.
Wherein especially is contained a compleat discourse and description of
The Four {Elements,
Constitutions,
Ages of Man,
Seasons of the Year.
Together with an Exact Epitomie of the Four Monarchies, viz.
The {Assyrian,
Persian,
Grecian,
Roman.
Also a Dialogue between Old England and New, concerning the late troubles.
With divers other pleasant and serious Poems.
By a Gentlewoman in those parts.
Printed at London for Stephen Bowtell at the signe of the Bible in Popes Head-Alley. 1650.

1650 First original work of poetry published from America, *The Tenth Muse Lately Sprung Up in America,* by "a Gentlewoman in those parts," Anne Bradstreet. She uses straightforward style to describe passionate griefs and loves. Poem to her husband: "If ever two were one, then surely we. / If ever man were loved by wife, then thee."

Colonial American Literature

Early secular works are limited to histories and accounts of life in the colonies, written to inform the British public. In the New England colonies, founded by zealots seeking to worship as they please without penalty, most writing is religious—sermons and tracts to edify and instruct the flock. Clergymen like Roger Williams and Thomas Hooker publish their views on theology. Even poetry preaches piety. The Metaphysical poems of the best Puritan poet, Edward Taylor, are not published until 200 years after his death. A Virginia planter, William Byrd, pens witty, coded diaries in secret. These lively records are not discovered until two centuries after he dies in 1744.

c. 1651 William Bradford publishes his history, *Of Plymouth Plantation*. Bradford describes colony as great experiment in epic account of Pilgrims' courage and endurance in face of adversity. Archetypal tale of early idealism,

difficulties, conflict, and dissolution of utopian mission. Theme: how the ideal founders when confronted with the real. Story told "in a plain style, with singular regard unto the simple truth." Scene in Bradford's house at Plymouth shows Pilgrims and Chief Massasoit agreeing to treaty, 1621.

1660 Samuel Pepys begins writing his private *Diary*, precursor of the prose novel with its recital of daily events. He continues for 9 years, but diary not published until it's deciphered in 1825. Written in cipher (system of shorthand), intended as private record, journal contains lively account of personalities, reflections, and domestic life in frank, intimate detail. "I went out to Charing Cross, to see Major-general Harrison hanged, drawn, quartered; which was done there, he looking as cheerful as any man could do in that condition." Pepys walks, wrapped protectively, through London street during Great Plague of 1665 in image.

1651 English political philosopher Thomas Hobbes publishes *Leviathan*. He consorts with leading intellects like Sir Francis Bacon, Ben Jonson, Galileo Galilei, and René Descartes, develops rationalist, materialist theory with utilitarian outlook. Examining nature and motion as 1st causes of human action, he concludes man is essentially selfish animal, in constant conflict with others. Writes in lucid prose employing effective metaphor and inventive irony. Calls man's life "solitary, poore, nasty, brutish and short."

1662 First poem published in North America is Michael Wigglesworth's "The Day of Doom." Harvard graduate and Massachusetts minister writes much poetry, full of apocalyptic predictions. "Day of Doom" is best-selling jeremiad, forecasts end of world, obliteration of human race due to moral backsliding. Didactic poem uses simple, cadenced rhythm to terrify reader into repenting.

The Mountains Smoak, the Hills are shook, the Earth is rent and torn,
As if she should be clean dissolv'd, or from the Center born.
The sea doth roar, forsakes the shore, and shrinks away for fear;
The wild Beasts flee into the Sea, so soon as he draws near.
                                        —Michael Wigglesworth, "Day of Doom"

1664 Molière writes scathing comedy *Tartuffe*, which satirizes fake piety. Playing the title role in his *The Imaginary Invalid*, Molière suffers hemorrhage after delivering closing lines, disguises condition with harsh laugh as curtain falls. (Shown, performance at Versailles.) Play attacks incompetence of physicians, mocks hypochondriac's fear of death. Conveyed home,

Molière admits, "My course is run," and dies. Before his run ends, Molière invents modern French comedy, ranging from absurd farce to ridicule that rivals tragedy in power. Attacks hypocrisy and pretension, promotes common sense and moderation.

1667 John Milton's most famous work, the epic, blank-verse poem *Paradise Lost*, describes fall of man. (Shown, Adam and Eve expelled from Paradise.) Aim is to "justifie the wayes of God to men." In 12 books, tells how Satan, a rebellious archangel, is exiled from heaven, then tempts Adam and Eve, who sin not from predestation but free will. With eloquent language, Milton, a Puritan and Humanist scholar, offers hope that humanity will be redeemed: "then wilt thou not be loath / To leave this Paradise, but shalt possess / A Paradise within thee, happier farr."

1667 French dramatist Jean Racine adapts Euripides's play in *Andromaque*. Tragedies are based on ancient history and biblical subjects. Racine strips away subplots and digressions, streamlines story to main action. His charac-

ters more closely resemble human beings than Corneille's. (For Corneille, tragedy deals with the extraordinary; Racine argues for realism.) Elegant, spare style opposed to bombast of the age. Explores depths of character revealed in action, not high-flown speeches. Shown, scene from *Esther*, tragedy Racine writes for girls' school sponsored by Madame de Maintenon, mistress of Louis XIV.

1678 John Dryden's blank-verse tragedy *All for Love* premieres in London, retells story of Antony and Cleopatra. Dryden champions heroic drama with exotic setting, lush violence, much commotion and excitement, a style Samuel Johnson calls "false magnificence." Besides dominating Restoration drama, Dryden writes poetry, such as satire *Absalom and Achitophel* (1681), using heroic couplet as termination to underline main point. He is known for his literary criticism, rendered in simple, direct style. As poet, playwright, translator, and critic, he dominates literary scene.

Restoration Drama

After being banned for 18 years (out of fear of moral contagion and literal transmission of the plague), theaters open again in England when the Stuarts regain the crown. In the interim, European drama flourished, and French Neoclassic dramatists like Corneille and Racine and Spanish playwrights Pedro Calderón de la Barca and Lope de Vega influence British theater. British drama becomes more international, less provincial, but also more clever than original, compared to the greatness of the Elizabethan theater. Writers like William Wycherley, William Congreve, and John Dryden present comedy-of-manners plays about frivolous gentlemen's affairs and shallow intrigues. Prose plays exude attitude of witty cynicism in complex plots full of repartee.

1688 First English philosophical novel by a woman, Aphra Behn's *Oroonoko, or the History of the Royal Slave*, an antislavery work, is published. Behn, who once served as a spy for King Charles II, visits Surinam (British Guiana), learns history of African prince Oroonoko and his love for Imoinde. Shown, Oronooko about to kill wife rather than see their child born in slavery. Behn is one of 1st female playwrights, writes 18 successful plays, and lives by her pen as the 1st professional female author in England.

1678 John Bunyan publishes allegorical *The Pilgrim's Progress*. Writes 9 books while in jail for preaching without a license. In Bunyan's most beloved book, a pilgrim named Christian leaves City of Destruction, wends way through sites that test his mettle like Slough of Despond and Valley of Humiliation to goal of Celestial City. Shown, Prudence, Discretion, Piety, and Charity arm Christian for struggle on his path. Simplicity and devotion of story garner wide audience.

The Wonders of the Invisible World:

Being an Account of the

TRYALS

OF

Several Witches,

Lately Executed in

NEW-ENGLAND:

And of several remarkable Curiosities therein Occurring.

Together with,

I. Observations upon the Nature, the Number, and the Operations of the Devils.
II. A short Narrative of a late outrage committed by a knot of Witches in Swede-Land, very much resembling, and so far explaining, that under which New-England has laboured.
III. Some Councels directing a due Improvement of the Terrible things lately done by the unusual and amazing Range of Evil-Spirits in New-England.
IV. A brief Discourse upon those Temptations which are the more ordinary Devices of Satan.

By COTTON MATHER.

Published by the Special Command of his EXCELLENCY the Governour of the Province of the Massachusetts-Bay in New-England.

Printed first, at Boston in New-England; and Reprinted at London, for John Dunton, at the Raven in the Poultry, 1693.

1693 Cotton Mather's book *The Wonders of the Invisible World* recounts Salem witch trials in 1692. Mather has an extraordinarily gifted mind. Enters Harvard at 12, performs brilliantly, writes more than 500 books on diverse subjects. Rails with fervor against heretics, condemning alleged witches as God's punishment for sinful New England. Filled with certainty of Puritans' divine mission.

From the Enlightenment and Age of Revolution to the Era of Evolution: Reason, Romance, Realism (1700–1900)

The major difference between the eighteenth century and first half of the nineteenth can be seen in gardens. The eighteenth century, called the Age of Reason or the Enlightenment, features gardens with ramrod-straight and orderly borders. Formal geometry is king. In contrast, the gardens of the Romantic era are ruled by emotional response, the desire to create a natural landscape that evokes the era's passion for nature—the wilder the better—and an enthusiasm for nostalgic ruins. Instead of tidy arrangements that discipline nature, Romantic gardens imitate the wilderness.

The Enlightenment, spread by philosophes like Denis Diderot, Voltaire, and John Locke, asserts the supremacy of human reason. Fostered by scientific discoveries, this Rationalist outlook holds that individuals and nations should be free of tyranny and that human reason should challenge assumptions about the authority of the church, state, and established institutions. In literature, this viewpoint exalts elegance, symmetry, proper form, and harmony. It harkens back to classical rules of self-restraint, moderation, self-discipline, and logic. The refined prose of essayists Joseph Addison, Richard Steele, and Samuel Johnson and the satire of Jonathan Swift and Alexander Pope are supreme products of this outlook.

In the political arena, these ideas give birth to the American colonies' war for independence from Great Britain. In 1789, in France, when King Louis XVI learns a mob has stormed the Bastille, he remarks, "This is a revolt." The messenger corrects him, "No, sire, it is a revolution." These momentous political changes end with the French king's beheading and the founding of a new republic on Enlightenment ideas of *liberté, fraternité*, and *égalité*. The same revolutionary ardor sweeps Latin America, and those liberation movements spell the end of absolute monarchy, paving the way for liberal, parliamentary governments.

Thanks to the Industrial Revolution, in full swing in the 1800s, life is transformed by new inventions and methods of production. Transportation accelerates after the first steamboat chugs up the Hudson River in 1805, and railroads and canals are constructed. Power-driven machines increase manufacturing, and inventions like the telegraph knit countries together and accelerate the spread of ideas. The electric motor, refrigeration, photography, mass production of steel, telephone, electric light, and discovery of oil push society into an urban, industrial, protomodern era. Although the American Civil War (1861–65) embroils the United States in violence, its outcome assures the triumph of the industrial model over the South's agrarian ways.

From about 1775 to 1850, an alternative current flows with increasing vigor: Romanticism. Romantic poets like Samuel Taylor Coleridge and William Wordsworth praise individualism, idealism, and revolt against rules and authority. Their writing is subjective, reveling in nature and sensibility. Jean-Jacques Rousseau and Johann Wolfgang von Goethe also fall into the camp of exaggerated Romanticism, lauding instinct, intuition, and worship of nature. For the first time, American literature comes of age, with Romantic Transcendentalists like Henry

David Thoreau, Walt Whitman, Nathaniel Hawthorne, and Herman Melville producing works of magisterial power.

Fyodor Dostoyevsky, Leo Tolstoy, and Ivan Turgenev exemplify sophisticated Russian literature. Turgenev pinpointed a nihilistic spirit that develops in the 1860s among Russian intelligentsia in a society dominated by Tsarist oppression. In his novel *Fathers and Sons* (1861), he defines the nihilist as "a man who does not bow down before any authority, who does not take any principle on faith, whatever reverence that principle may be enshrined in." In short, nothing is sacred, and a "go to the people" missionary movement develops, in which young Russian aristocrats and university students work alongside peasants. Karl Marx's theories increasingly inspire adherents of socialism and the growth of labor movements.

Around the 1840s, when the Victorian era is in full swing in England, technological advances produce material prosperity among the upper and middle classes. A mood of smug complacency prevails, caught in optimistic, sentimental, ornate poetry by Alfred, Lord Tennyson and Robert Browning. The moralistic tone is evident in Browning's "God's in his heaven— / All's right with the world."

But all is not quite right. Since the Enclosure Act around 1750 drove peasants off the land and into increasingly crowded cities, British cities become squalid, smoky hellholes. London grows from a population of one million in 1801 to seven million in 1911. In the 1890s, 30 percent of London's inhabitants live in poverty.

Child labor screams for reform, and Charles Dickens comes to the fore with novels of social protest.

In terms of material prosperity and rising standards of living, the nineteenth century is a Golden Age in Europe. Life is enhanced by mass production and breakthroughs against disease by scientists like Louis Pasteur. It's also a Golden Age for the novel. In England, Jane Austen, Charlotte, Emily and Anne Brontë, George Eliot, and Thomas Hardy produce masterpieces alongside Dickens. In France, it's Honoré de Balzac, Gustave Flaubert, Victor Hugo, and Émile Zola, and in the United States, besides Hawthorne and Melville, Henry James, William Dean Howells, and Mark Twain are at the top of their craft.

After about 1860 novels shift in their outlook from Romanticism to Realism. Influenced by Darwin's theory of natural selection (published in 1859), writers look on life as a struggle for survival. Their works document social, environmental, and biological forces that impinge on human destiny. In the extreme form of Realism called Naturalism, mankind engages in a fight to the finish.

As the century comes to a close, the certainties of Victorian morality are increasingly eroded by a conflict between science and religion. Despite all the progress and prosperity of the nineteenth century, its heyday is effectively over with the outbreak of World War I in 1914, fueled by narrow nationalism, militarism, and economic imperialism. As the British foreign secretary Edward Grey describes his feelings just before England enters the Great War: "The lamps are going out all over Europe; we shall not see them lit again in our life-time."

1700 British dramatist William Congreve's *The Way of the World*, comic masterpiece of polished speechifying and subtle characterization, is performed. Although highly popular, Congreve offends middle-class prudery, retires from writing plays at 30. *The Way of the World*,

stronger in witty dialogue than action, offers cynical peek beneath upper-class glamour. "To drink is a Christian diversion unknown to the Turk and the Persian." When world-renowned philosopher Voltaire visits, Congreve insists his literary worth is zilch, to which Voltaire replies, "In that sad case, you would not have received a visit from me."

1709 Joseph Addison and Richard Steele perfect the elegant essay in periodicals *The Tatler* and *The Spectator*. Both use device of fictional authors—urbane, erudite observers—who comment on London society. Goal: "to enliven morality with wit, and to temper wit with morality." Essays promote proper behavior, pronounce verdict on literature of the day. Steele denounces bawdy Restoration drama: "I allow it to be Nature, but it is Nature in its utmost Corruption and Degeneracy." Neoclassic ideal is "sober and polite Mirth." Immensely popular periodicals set the style for aristocratic English during 18th century.

The SPECTATOR.

1712 Alexander Pope's *The Rape of the Lock* (Aubrey Beardsley's cover design shown) sets standard for mock-heroic verse. Playful epic parodies

2 feuding families of polite society by poking fun at young lady whose lock of hair is purloined by an aspiring lover. *The Dunciad* (1728–42) is scathing satire, brimming with witty irony and vicious attacks on authors ("a brain of feathers, and a heart of lead") who criticize Pope's work. Pope is called Wicked Wasp of Twickenham for his poison-pen style. As Romantic currents increase, his Neoclassic style comes to be seen as artificial and overly refined.

1719 *Robinson Crusoe* by Daniel Defoe is 1st long tale to appear serially, tells story of shipwrecked mariner with his "Man Friday," a native with whom sailor contends against cannibals. Defoe, a prolific writer and reporter, world traveler, spy, and breeder of civet cats, hits his literary stride at nearly age 60 with *Robinson Crusoe*. Based on a true story, considerably embellished, of privateer stranded on island; tells of survivor's ingenuity. Plain prose is packed with realistic detail and gripping narrative; popular story creates enduring myth. (Shown, N. C. Wyeth's illustration of Crusoe.) In 1722, Defoe's pic-aresque (episodic) *Moll Flanders* and fictional *A Journal of the Plague Year* appear. *Moll Flanders*, forerunner of modern novel, is one of 1st social novels, purports to be autobiography of pickpocket and harlot.

1726 Jonathan Swift's *Gulliver's Travels* satirizes contemporary world through tale of hero's experiences with tiny Lilliputians, giants, and ultrarational horses, contrasted to loutish Yahoos (beasts in human form).

Tiny scale of Lilliputians renders ridiculous the pompous officials—stand-ins for petty, English politicians—and their feuds. In Brobdingnag, inhabitants tall as steeples conclude that Gulliver's people are "the most pernicious race of little odious vermin that nature ever suffered to crawl upon the surface of the earth." Only among the Houyhnhnms, a race of sensible horses, does Gulliver find true civilization. Swift's 1729 pamphlet "A Modest Proposal," masterpiece of deadpan irony, suggests remedy for Irish famine: raising children as victuals ("stewed, roasted, baked or boiled").

Birth of the Novel

Both Richardson's *Pamela* and Fielding's *Tom Jones* are often termed the 1st true English novels, as distinguished from 17th-century prose romances called "histories," precursors of the modern novel. From memoirs and fictionalized epistolary narratives in prose, the modern novel develops into the dominant form using an omniscient, 3rd-person narrator. Other early 18th-century practitioners like Daniel Defoe, Tobias Smollett, and Laurence Sterne elaborate the genre, varying its style and subject matter. By the early 19th century, Jane Austen's novels show full-blown mastery, while Sir Walter Scott extends the novel into historical settings. Later 19th-century writers continue to expand their novels of manners and morals. William Makepeace Thackeray, Eliot, Dickens, Anthony Trollope, and Hardy dissect society realistically and didactically. In contrast, the Brontë sisters pursue a romantic direction, while Robert Louis Stevenson uses the long form to launch adventure tales.

1740 Samuel Richardson's *Pamela* is considered the 1st modern English novel. Prototype of "epistolary novel" is told through letters from heroine and journal entries. Richardson, an industrious printer, publisher, and writer, finishes novel in 2 months. Work is widely praised for its realism and moral message, as well as the immediacy of its style, which Richardson calls "writing to the moment." Story tells of comely 15-year-old servant girl, Pamela, pursued by lecherous nobleman. Pamela strives mightily to retain her chastity, and her virtue is rewarded when she marries the reformed rake, shown. Richardson's later epistolary novel *Clarissa* longest novel in English at 1 million words, expands depth of novel through interest in psychological aspects of character.

1749 One of finest comic novels ever, *The History of Tom Jones, a Foundling,* by Henry Fielding, is published. Called "an accomplished blackguard" by Lord Byron, Tom is an appealing rascal, a roguish hero who blithely endures ignoble trials. Story tells of foundling Tom, reared in prosperous home of Squire Allworthy. The squire's malicious nephew turns Allworthy against lusty Tom. Through many misadventures, Tom pursues his true love, Sophia, until the secret of his parentage reveals Allworthy to be his uncle. Arguably the 1st modern novelist, Fielding (seen in portrait by William Hogarth) considers himself "the founder of a new province of writing." Original and innovative, he departs from epistolary model to create "comic epics in prose."

1751 Thomas Gray meditates on mortality and rural life in "Elegy Written in a Country Churchyard," one of most popular poems of 18th century. Melancholy reflection on dignity of unknown poor who are buried in church cemetery, seen in illustration, contains some of

best-known lines in poetry, like "Full many a flower is born to blush unseen." On vanity of human life, British poet concludes, "the paths of glory lead but to the grave." Poem foreshadows Romantic movement in love of nature, moody nostalgia. In "Ode on a Distant Prospect of Eton College," Gray notes, "Where ignorance is bliss, / 'Tis folly to be wise." His aim in poetry is "extreme conciseness of expression, yet pure, perspicuous, and musical."

Literature of the Enlightenment

The Enlightenment, or Age of Reason, is more an attitude than a set of ideas. Founded on the strides made in the physical sciences by the 1730s, this worldview entails a general questioning of authority, convention, religious dogma, and morals. Nature, considered through the lens of science, is seen to follow laws discernible by reason. According to the secular belief called Deism, God is viewed as a hands-off clockmaker who merely initiated the action of the universe. Writers associated with the Enlightenment, which is soundly entrenched in the mainstream of European thought by the 1780s, include Rousseau and Voltaire. Pope expresses the new secular emphasis on the natural world, self-interest, and logic: "Know then thyself, presume not God to scan / The proper study of mankind is man." In literature, it's an age of prose, the development of the novel, and brilliant satire, such as the works of Jonathan Swift and Voltaire. The work that epitomizes the era is Denis Diderot's 35-volume *Encyclopedia*, attempting to sum up all knowledge and dispel superstition.

1755 Samuel Johnson, known as Dr. Johnson (seen in portrait by his friend Joshua Reynolds), publishes *A Dictionary of the English Language* in 2 volumes. Monumental work, 1st of its kind in English, standard reference for decades, defines more than 40,000 words, illustrated with 114,000 quotations. Johnson, most eminent literary figure in England during 2nd half of 18th century, believes human happiness is impossible in an imperfect world. A brilliant talker who makes conversation a competitive art form, Johnson spouts aphorisms as a fire sprays sparks. Examples: "Let me smile with the wise and feed with the rich," and "He who praises everybody praises nobody." Speaking of a man who remarried immediately after his 1st shrewish wife died, Johnson quips, "the triumph of hope over experience."

1759 Voltaire's short, satiric novel *Candide* satirizes philosopher Gottfried Leibniz's naïve belief that, as Candide's tutor Dr. Pangloss insists, "all is for the best in this best of all possible worlds." In drama, essays, and poetry, Voltaire expresses aversion to organized religion and spreads new scientific ideas. A merciless enemy of injustice and intolerance, Voltaire is most famous French thinker of his day. Polemical letters criticize authority ("If God did not exist, it would be necessary to invent him"). He's best known for character Candide, who, with his beloved Cunégonde (shown, the two marrying) suffers 1 misfortune after the other while Dr. Pangloss declares everything is rosy. At end, Candide pronounces secret of happiness: "We must cultivate our own garden."

1759 Laurence Sterne's unique *The Life and Opinions of Tristram Shandy, Gentleman* breaks all rules with its chaotic style, is regarded as forerunner of stream-of-consciousness novel. Sterne is British pastor, violinist, womanizer, and audacious innovator of prose fiction. Sterne has well-developed sense of the absurd and a bawdy wit. *Tristram Shandy*

remains a 1-of-a-kind, nonsensical delight. Erratic narration is interrupted by flagrant digressions, its sequence of events is deliberately violated, and its plot is nonexistent. Sterne plays with typography and layout, incorporating flourishes of asterisks, dashes, and miscellaneous typefaces. On a blank page, he invites reader to write own description of Widow Wadman, shown here with Shandy's Uncle Toby. Sterne cheerfully undercuts illusion of reality the novel promotes.

1761 Swiss-born philosopher Jean-Jacques Rousseau publishes *Julie ou la Nouvelle Héloïse* (*Julie, or the New Heloise*), exalts natural man and denigrates hypocritical morality. His *Émile, ou l'Education* (*Emile, or On Education*, 1762) is about rearing boys according to principles of nature, with physical exercise and learning through observation and experience. Book is widely influential. A man of

contradictions, Rousseau states aim of education is self-expression and that development of pupil is supremely important. Meanwhile, he consigns his own 5 children by a common-law wife to an orphanage. Rousseau is considered father of French Romanticism for his glorification of nature, rebellious individualism, and emphasis on imagination and emotion. Most important work of social theory, *The Social Contract* (1762), begins: "Man is born free and is everywhere in chains."

1764 Horace Walpole writes 1st Gothic novel *The Castle of Otranto*, setting vogue for supernatural tales and "purple prose." Son of wealthy British prime minister, Walpole begins life as dedicated partygoer fond of lace collars and luxury, a dilettante and witty letter writer. His true passion is for Gothic Revival architecture and medieval lore, the setting for his Gothic tales. Over 40 years, he transforms cottage overlooking Thames into 30-room, faux-haunted, Gothic castle. Strawberry Hill, seen here, is adorned with battlements, crenellated

towers, a cloister, and armory. This devotee of funereal gloom is so enthusiastic for clanking chains and moonlit graveyards of ghost stories, he decorates his living room with a tomb. Walpole's lightly ironic, voluminous correspondence establishes him as "the best informed gossip of his century."

The Gothic Novel: Thrills and Chills

Following the success of Walpole's *Castle of Otranto*, authors dip their pens in the well of doom and gloom and produce supernatural tales set in creepy cemeteries, ruined abbeys, and haunted castles leaking blood. The Gothic novel reaches a pinnacle of popularity in the late 1790s and early 19th century. The genre includes macabre tales by British novelist Ann Radcliffe (*The Mysteries of Udolpho,* 1794), Irish author Maria Edgeworth (*Castle Rackrent*, 1800), and the American Charles Brockden Brown (*Arthur Mervyn*, 1799). Later, Mary Shelley and the Brontë sisters explore the delicious terrors of solitude, with vivid descriptions of picturesque landscapes that mirror characters' agitated mood. Wild plots, suspense, and fear enrapture readers, showing the dark side of human life: obsession, seduction, and cruelty. (Cue a demonic, blood-curdling cackle.) The actress Sarah Bernhardt is so taken with Gothic romance, she sleeps in a coffin.

1766 Irishman Oliver Goldsmith's popular pastoral novel *The Vicar of Wakefield* is published. His play *She Stoops to Conquer* (1773) is success. Goldsmith, a vain, awkward, and ridiculous figure in society, leaves these 2

works and one poem in the permanent canon of literature. His poem "The Deserted Village" (1770), about peasants' loss of their homes, contains line: "Ill fares the land, to hastening ills a prey, / Where wealth accumulates, and men decay." Goldsmith is a flashy dresser, profligate gambler, and lavish spender who supports himself on loans from friends and playing the flute. After Goldsmith's death, Samuel Johnson counters: "Let not his frailties be remembered; he was a very great man." Joshua Reynolds, who painted Goldsmith's portrait (shown), says: "Wherever he was there was no yawning."

1771 Tobias Smollett's *The Expedition of Humphrey Clinker* is published shortly before his death. Satiric epistolary novel details tumultuous, comic events throughout invalid's travels. Smollett, a medical doctor who believed the 4 "humors," or fluids, are responsible for physical conditions, portrays his characters as simplified exemplars of various eccentricities. Exaggerated characters transmit broad, scathing satire bordering on burlesque. The Scottish author wishes to incite "that generous indignation which ought to animate the reader against the sordid and vicious disposition of the world."

1771 Benjamin Franklin's charming memoir *Autobiography* offers tips on life well lived. His homilies like "Early to bed and early to rise" in *Poor Richard's Almanac* (1732) advise prudence, industry, and frugality. Franklin, 15th child of a poor Boston candlemaker, exemplifies American dream of self-made man. Begins as printer's apprentice. At age 17, he runs off with only 1 Dutch dollar and a shilling to Philadelphia, where he makes his name and fortune. Helps shape destiny of nation through Declaration of Independence, pamphlets urging self-government, and U.S. Constitution. *Autobiography* is popular, written in simple, direct style, preaches doctrine of self-reliance. In it, this archetypal man of the Enlightenment outlines his personal project for moral improvement.

1774 Johann Wolfgang von Goethe's semi-autobiographical *The Sorrows of Young Werther* is huge success. In sentimental tale, young man (shown with his true love) kills himself with rival's pistol after being rejected by his beloved. Powerful, exaggerated emotion causes wave of spurned suitors throughout Europe to commit suicide. His innovative 1773 play, *Götz von Berlichingen* (*With the Iron Hand*), sets stage for emotive style known as *Sturm und Drang* (*Storm and Stress*), featuring Promethean individual who fights social injustice to bring needed reforms. Goethe's *Wilhelm Meister's Apprenticeship* (1795) establishes genre of *Bildungsroman*, a coming-of-age tale. In *Faust*, a philosophical verse drama, the scholar Faust makes pact with devil, is saved by angelic choir singing, "He who exerts himself in constant striving, / Him we can save."

1775 Irish-born Richard Brinsley Sheridan is 24 when his 1st, archly comic play, *The Rivals*, opens in London. Hilarious Mrs. Malaprop garbles words, praising a character as "the very pineapple of politeness." *School for Scandal* is classic satire lampooning high-society gossipmongers. Sheridan deflates pomposity and devises intricate comic situations and unforgettable characters. Although he enters Parliament after meteoric stint as playwright, he's still known for one-liners. When Drury Lane Theater, which he co-owns, burns, Sheridan watches fire from neighboring pub. When a friend remarks on his composure, Sheridan quips, "A man may surely take a glass of wine by his own fireside." Shown, John Gielgud (left) as Joseph Surface and Ralph Richardson as Sir Peter Teazle in *School for Scandal*.

1776 Rabble-rouser Thomas Paine shows power of words in pamphlet "Common Sense," a rallying cry for American independence from Britain. Radical British propagandist recommends freedom and self-government. His forceful rhetorical style enflames resentment over English oppression, inspires colonists to revolt. After George Washington is defeated in New York, Paine rallies rebel spirits with words: "These are the times that try men's souls" and expresses scorn for "the summer soldier and the sunshine patriot." Paine, a consummate agitator, opposes hereditary monarch in England in his "Rights of Man" (1791) pamphlet. His political theories do not express a systematic philosophy but passionately oppose tyranny to inspire change.

The Lone Ranger

Between 1775 and 1850, the concept of the artist as a romantic hero develops in literature. The hero, as portrayed by Goethe, is typically an outsider who gushes about the grandeur of nature and the glory of antiquity. He rejects convention and searches for truth and heightened sensory experience. The myth of the misunderstood, starving artist transforms the writer's role from an ironic observer to that of a bohemian genius on the margins of society. Later, patterned on the life and writing of the poet Lord Byron, the archetype of the Byronic hero (a passionate, suffering, superhuman outcast, driven by demons to confront titanic forces) influences 19th-century literature and thought. Although doomed, the hero rebels against injustice and refuses to bow to overwhelming power. He triumphs—if only in asserting the freedom of his will—as in Byron's description of Childe Harold: "When fortune fled her spoiled and favorite child, / He stood unbowed beneath the ills upon him piled."

1776 Edward Gibbon begins publishing his vast (and vastly popular) 1,000-year survey *The History of the Decline and Fall of the Roman Empire*. British scholar debunks legend of Rome as pinnacle of civilization. Although he details many achievements, he shows Roman Empire was doomed to fail because of chauvinism and fallible leaders infected with pride. Stresses need for strong institutions to curb selfishness, human folly, and collective error. Sonorous, polished sentences embody rational spirit, although a wit remarked it would be useful to translate Gibbon into English. Gibbon, whose caricature is shown here, finishes the 71st chapter, a labor of 20 years, in 1788.

1782 Beloved German writer Friedrich von Schiller slips away from regiment where he serves as army surgeon to watch performance of his 1st play *Die Räuber* (The Robbers). Duke has him thrown in brig, orders him to refrain from

writing plays. Schiller absconds, suffers in poverty until he writes *Don Carlos* in 1787, which wins acclaim. Becomes friends with Goethe, who encourages him to incorporate historical subjects. *William Tell* (1804), his last play, a stirring rejection of tyranny, considered best. Also known for works in *Sturm und Drang* movement, and essays and lyric poetry. Considers poet like priest, whose idealistic, impassioned rhetoric should inspire readers with grandeur of humanity. Beethoven sets poem "Ode to Joy" to music.

1787 British schoolmarm Mary Wollstonecraft calls for education of women in *Thoughts on the Education of Daughters*. Her most famous work is *A Vindication of the Rights of Women* (1792). Author attacks "mistaken notions" that keep women in "ignorance and slavish dependence," denying them proper education. She asserts that prejudice forces women to be unin-

formed and passive, denying them both mental and physical stimulation and preventing intellectual growth by requiring docility. "From the tyranny of man . . . the greater number of female follies proceed." Some rally to support her, while conservative Horace Walpole denounces her as "a hyena in petticoats." Wollstonecraft marries anarchic philosopher William Godwin; she dies shortly after giving birth to daughter, the future Mary Shelley.

1787 Scottish national poet Robert Burns publishes "Auld Lang Syne" in Scottish dialect and "Red, Red Rose," with the opening line, "O my Luve's like a red, red rose, / That's newly sprung in June; O My Luve's like the melodie / That's sweetly play'd in tune." Born in a hut, he works on a farm while reading constantly. Addicted to the ladies, he admits, "My heart was completely tinder, and was eternally lighted

up by some Goddess or other." He fathers 9 illegitimate children. To finance his escape from angry fathers and tearful maids, he publishes poems in Scots dialect. Burns is proclaimed a "native genius" of "untutored fancy," becomes professional poet. Assumes persona of illiterate plowman, but poems are more than "wild effusions of the heart."

1789 William Blake publishes poems, including "Spring" (shown), in *Songs of Innocence*, illustrated with his own engravings. English Romantic poet sees angels in the trees, their wings shining like gold, and speaks to spirits. He maintains his poems are "dictated" and paintings are "copied" from visions. A missionary for realm of imagination, Blake prints poems himself in "an Endeavor to Restore . . . the Golden Age." Poems, conceived visually, unify text and image: "How the chimney-sweeper's cry / Every black'ning church appalls; / And the hapless soldier's sigh / Runs in blood down palace walls" (from "London"). He welcomes death in 1827 as opportunity to join spirit world, with which he'd long communed.

1791 James Boswell publishes *The Life of Samuel Johnson*, establishing gold standard for biography. Caricature shows Boswell talking to his idol "till near two in the morning," absorbing the master conversationalist's anecdotes. Intimate portrait reveals larger-than-life personality of celebrated writer, whom Boswell shadows for more than 20 years, collecting material. Dr. Johnson virtually leaps from page full-blown, lively and erudite, opinionated and garrulous. When Johnson tells Boswell, "Well, we had a good talk," Boswell replies gleefully, "Yes, Sir; you tossed and gored several persons."

Romantic Poetry in England

The period 1775–1830 is an age of revolution: the American and French Revolutions, the beginning of the Industrial Revolution (especially in England), and a revolution in art and ways of thinking. As egalitarian ideas sweep the West, Wordsworth writes of "France standing on the top of golden hours / And human nature seeming born again." The period from the end of the 18th century to 1830 is called the Romantic Era. Its chief glory in literature is British poetry by Wordsworth, Coleridge, Shelley, Byron, and Keats. Reacting against the Neoclassical taste for reason and regularity during the 18th-century Enlightenment, writers embrace nature, self-revelation, and strong emotion. "Poetry," as Wordsworth defines it, "is the spontaneous overflow of powerful feelings." Picturesque, exotic imagery, subjectivity, and a yearning, striving spirit run rampant through Romantic verse. Imagination and intuition are the vehicles to liberate and regenerate mankind for the poet who, as Coleridge says, "brings the whole soul of man into activity."

1800

1798 *Lyrical Ballads* by William Wordsworth and Samuel Taylor Coleridge is 1st major work of English Romantic period. Includes Coleridge's "Rime of the Ancient Mariner" and Wordsworth's "Lines Composed a Few Miles Above Tintern Abbey." Coleridge produces major poems ("Ancient Mariner" and fragmentary "Christabel" and "Kubla Khan") during 18 months of close friendship with Wordsworth. Coleridge, known as dazzling talker, transforms "conversation poem," which springs from moment in everyday life and forges intimate relation between speaker and audience. "Ancient Mariner" is colloquial masterpiece of psychological and philosophical depth. Sailor, who errs through wanton killing of albatross (seen in engraving by Gustave Doré), must expiate guilt by confessing crime before he's redeemed by discovering, "He prayeth well, who loveth well / both man and bird and beast."

1807 William Wordsworth publishes famous poems "I Wandered Lonely as a Cloud" (hailing "a host, of golden daffodils": "Ten Thousand saw I at a glance, / Tossing their heads in sprightly dance") and "Ode: Intimations of Immortality" ("Though nothing can bring back the hour / Of splendour in the grass, of glory in the flower; / We will grieve not, rather find / Strength in what remains behind.") Poems describe a particular scene vividly, then jump to an epiphany based on the vignette. Truths glimpsed in nature evolve into mature beliefs. In "Tintern Abbey," Nature forms moral character: "While with an eye made quiet by the power / Of harmony, and the deep power of joy, / We see into the life of things."

1811 Jane Austen's 1st published novel, *Sense and Sensibility*, appears. *Pride and Prejudice* (rejected for publication when written in 1796) published in 1813. Shown, its feisty heroine Elizabeth Bennet meets supercilious Mr.

Darcy, accompanied by two snobs. Austen, one of the greatest English novelists, satirizes manners of both country and city folk in polished style brimming with human comedy. Cast of characters set in provinces includes sharp portraits of obsequious fools, hoity-toity matrons, society-obsessed gentlemen, finagling mothers, indulgent fathers, and quick-witted heroines. Vivid characters and their brilliant conversation make novels delightful reading.

1812 George Gordon, Lord Byron, writes wildly popular epic poem *Childe Harold's Pilgrimage*, which recounts melancholy hero's solitary wanderings through Europe and establishes Byron as heartthrob of Europe. "Mad, bad, and dangerous to know," his lover Lady Caroline Lamb describes the dashingly handsome aristocrat. A cult of adoring fans lionizes Byron, after

his melodramatic, escapist travelogue appears. Epic poems invent the prototypical Romantic hero, who wanders abroad, jaded from pleasure, infected by secret sorrow. From the height of fame, Byron falls to infamy when rumor spreads of his incest with half-sister. Scandal causes high society to shun him, and he seeks refuge in Europe to compose finest works: *Manfred, Childe Harold IV*, and the satiric *Beppo* and *Don Juan*. Sensational language describes battle of Waterloo: "How that red rain hath made the harvest grow!" Byron dies aiding Greeks in revolt against Turks.

1814 Sir Walter Scott's *Waverly* is 1st of his series of popular historical novels featuring Scottish lairds in tartan kilts. Scott is interested in old Scottish Border tales and ballads at early age; gives up narrative poetry for prolific career as Romantic novelist. He establishes historical novel as an

accepted genre, treating regional themes in local speech. *Rob Roy* (1818) introduces Scottish Robin Hood type. *Ivanhoe* (1819) is romantic tale of Saxon knight in Norman England. (Shown, Ivanhoe's heroine, Rebecca, being carried off by Crusaders in painting by Delacroix.) *Ivanhoe* presents colorful picture of medieval pageantry: knights' tournaments and besieged castle engulfed in flames. Despite his contrived plots, Scott, known as the Wizard of the North, is most popular novelist of his day.

1817 "Thanatopsis" by William Cullen Bryant is 1st mature poem published in U.S. Bryant, who began to compose verse at age 8, prays while still a child for "the gift of poetic genius" and to "write verses that might endure." He's now known mainly for this poem influenced by British "graveyard" poets dealing with emotions of bereavement and longing for immortality. Bryant is 1st native-born American poet to be celebrated internationally. Romantic poems praise American landscape as

healer and teacher. Bryant excels as editor of New York *Evening Post* newspaper; leaves estate of $1 million at death in 1878.

1818 Mary Wollstonecraft Shelley is author of *Frankenstein,* 1st science-fiction novel. Shelley claims concept derives from nightmare after she, her

husband (poet Percy Bysshe Shelley), and fellow poet Lord Byron spend rainy summer near Geneva reading ghost stories. Gothic tale concerns university student, Frankenstein, who discovers secret of life. He animates monster, a semblance of a human being constructed from spare parts scavenged from graves and anatomy class. Lonely, mistreated creature turns evil, wreaking vengeance on his creator who usurped God's prerogative. Reverent descriptions of nature indebted to influence of English Romantic poets.

1819 John Keats writes immortal poems such as "Ode to a Nightingale" before he dies at age 25 (shown, his life mask). The English poet most often compared to Shakespeare for his genius in melodious phrase making and sympathy for humanity, Keats publishes 1st book of poetry at age 22. Racked by tuberculosis, Keats despairs at not fulfilling his literary hopes, begs that his grave bear no name, only, "Here lies one whose name was writ in water." Keats's poetry exposes diverse points of view without simplistic resolution. Odes begin cheerfully, rise to intense joy, then regress to awareness of actuality. In "Ode on a Grecian Urn," he celebrates immortality of art that captures beauty of panting lovers: "She cannot fade though thou hast not thy bliss, / Forever wilt thou love, and she be fair."

1819 Washington Irving creates American legends like tale of Ichabod Crane in *The Legend of Sleepy Hollow* and *Rip Van Winkle* (shown). Irving is 1st American fiction writer to win world acclaim, or, as William Makepeace Thackeray says, "the 1st Ambassador whom the New World of Letters sent to the Old." His later fiction is filled with Gothic touches of ghosts and supernatural events. In his work modeled on English mentors, Irving treats American source material as picturesque and poetic, worthy of high literature. Irving's tales and sketches approximate short stories, although more akin to extended anecdotes in structure. An important figure in development of a national literature.

1820 Romantic Percy Bysshe Shelley's poems "To a Skylark" and "The Cloud" glorify nature. A flaming revolutionary with ethereal good looks, at age 18 Shelley is expelled from Oxford University after he sends his essay "The Necessity of Atheism" to all professors and bishops. He fails on next quest to transform Ireland into "the society of peace and love." Undaunted, at age 19 he distributes pamphlet "Declaration of Rights" by sticking text in bottles cast into ocean and sending others aloft with balloons. Shelley lives according to his ideals of justice and emancipation for women. Produces some of the most beautiful lyric poems in England and dies by drowning at age 29. On his gravestone is epitaph *Cor cordium*, "heart of hearts."

Poetry in (E)motion

Percy Shelley's poetry employs concrete, direct language and imagery, passionate singing rhythm, and original metaphors that bloom into abstract symbols. His technique involves finite words that ascend to the infinite. Gradually Shelley realizes society will only improve when humanity is regenerated through stirring individuals' hearts, through art, to love. He calls this goal "transforming enlargements of the imagination." Matthew Arnold calls him a "beautiful and ineffectual angel, beating in the void his luminous wings in vain." Ever the optimist, Shelley concludes "To the West Wind" with the line, "If Winter comes, can Spring be far behind?"

1823 James Fenimore Cooper publishes *The Pioneers*, 1st in series featuring woodsman Natty Bumppo, also called Pathfinder or Hawkeye (in *The Last of the Mohicans*, 1826). Cooper invents myth of frontier in 5 Leatherstocking novels featuring archetypal Western hero. Books are best sellers, appealing to Americans' desire for stories about their experience. James Russell Lowell criticizes his sentimental heroines as "sappy as maples and flat as a prairie." But Cooper is innovator who creates both genre of maritime, historical novel and memorable frontiersman hero. Deerslayer, seen in N. C. Wyeth's illustration, is emblem of goodness. He struggles against encroaching civilization with all its complicating, corrupting influences. Themes of loss of simplicity in New Eden and of "noble savage" resonate.

1822 Italian Alessandro Manzoni's novel *I Promessi sposi* (*The Betrothed*) is considered one of Italy's finest. Major work by leading Romantic writer is historical novel, which synthesizes fact, imagination, and poetic moralizing. A devout Catholic and patriot, Manzoni aims to illustrate workings of divine providence in affairs of common man. In novel, although local aristocrat opposes marriage of 2 peasants, goodness and happy ending prevail. Language is a refined precedent of modern Italian prose.

1827 Heinrich Heine's early poems in *Buch der Lieder* (*The Book of Songs*) contain famous ballad on Lorelei theme. (Shown, Lorelei, a siren who lures ships to destruction with her singing.) Heine, one of greatest German lyric poets, abandons conservative Prussian state for exile in Paris. His Romantic poems mix irony with satire. Combines wit and sentiment, lucidity and strength in folk songs notable for their easy, flexible rhymes and rhythm. Poems are often epigrammatic and occasionally acerbic. Love poems, especially from *Lyrisches Intermezzo* (*The Lyrical Intermezzo*, 1822–23), seem Romantic, with their apostrophes to love, but ambivalence and skepticism are latent. Poems revel in enjoyment of Romantic emotionalism, while undercutting ideal with glint of reality.

1830 Stendhal, one of greatest French writers, publishes acclaimed psychological novel *Le Rouge et le Noir* (*The Red and the Black*). Although his plots and subjects are Romantic and melodramatic, Stendhal is forerunner of modern novel through psychological probing and realistic treatment of character. Analyzes his egotistical protagonists, who struggle amid love and war, to discover their inner states. In *The Red and the Black*, Stendhal subjects sensitive youth Julien Sorel to acute character analysis. His masterpiece, *La Chartreuse de Parme* (*The Charterhouse of Parma*, 1839), also features a passionate hero who pursues love and power.

1831 Victor Hugo's most famous novel, *Notre-Dame de Paris* (*The Hunchback of Notre Dame*), portrays deformed bell ringer Quasimodo's

devotion to the beautiful Esmeralda, shown. Romance, set in Notre Dame cathedral during Middle Ages, reveals Hugo's compassion for suffering humanity. Quasimodo saves Esmeralda from mob after evil archdeacon denounces her as a witch. When she's executed unjustly, Quasimodo throws villain from belltower. Hugo is leading French Romantic writer of melancholy lyric poetry and humanitarian novels and plays. In 1830, his play *Hernani* ushers in new age in French theater with its controversial form and content. Hugo innovates by mixing comic and tragic elements, uses everyday speech instead of following formal rules of French Neoclassic drama. Theatergoers riot.

1832 George Sand's semiautobiographical novel *Indiana* wins notoriety with its stand on free love for both men and women. "It astonishes me," the novelist Gustave Flaubert says of the Frenchwoman who takes the pen name George Sand, "that you haven't died 20 times, you've thought so much, written so much, suffered so much." Sand's extravagant erotic life is nearly as prolific as her literary output (80 novels, written in haste). Sand is known as both a cigar-smoking lesbian dressed as "a dashing man about town" and a nymphomaniac whose serial lovers include the composer Frédéric Chopin and poet Alfred de Musset. (Shown, Musset's drawing of Sand.) Her novels reflect the same headlong gusto with which she lives her life.

George Sand: A Singular Sensation

George Sand revolts against authority by dressing as a cigar-chomping man and protesting the evils of loveless, arranged marriages, of which she was a victim. Sand addresses social problems in her novels, cloaked in romantic melodrama. Fyodor Dostoyevsky calls her "a clairvoyant seer" and Ivan Turgenev "one of our saints," but Sand considers most men useless, "*l'homme inutile*"—all talk and no action, a much-discussed concept in the mid-19th century, when Russian intellectuals endlessly chatted about revolution but continued to live off their serfs. After she obtains a legal separation from her husband, Sand must write to make a living and becomes the most prolific female writer of all time. Given her obsessive work habits, one of her defenders refutes the charge that Sand engages in orgies, saying she has no time for dalliance. But dally she does, and her notorious novels are full of women who follow their hearts to indulge in adultery and *menage à trois.* "What debases a woman is the lie," one of her characters remarks. "What constitutes adultery is not the hour that she grants her lover but the night that she will then spend in her husband's arms." After Sand dies in 1876, the French Senate bans her writings, except for her tame "grandmother stories" of country life.

1832 Preeminent Victorian poet Alfred, Lord Tennyson publishes *Poems* including Arthurian parable "The Lady of Shalott." Popular "Locksley Hall" portrays despondent hero, while "Ulysses" (1842) ends with robust manifesto: "Made weak by time and fate but strong in will / To strive, to seek, to find, and not to yield." Tennyson becomes poet laureate of England in 1850, assumes public role as prophet and teacher. Although themes of loneliness and despair dominate his poetry, he urges moral responsibility. Poems vacillate between expressing an individual vision of sensual beauty, using lyrical imagery to create poignant mood, and the necessity of dealing with social problems. "In Memoriam" (1850), long elegy for a friend who died young, is his greatest poem and embodies conflict between sensual world and spirit.

1833 Romantic poet Aleksandr Pushkin publishes masterpiece *Yevgeny Onegin* (*Eugene Onegin*), verse novel about shallow hero, Eugene—aloof, indecisive, and socially useless—and ideal heroine Tatyana. Book is his most important work and is immensely influential in Russian literature. Pushkin introduces rough, simple, concise language in modern Russian poetry, rejecting French Neoclassic style. Called the "Byron of Russia" for the riotous excesses of his personal life, his poetic excellence, and his stand against tyranny. His historical drama *Boris Godunov*, in which a czar is tortured by guilt after murdering a rival, is banned by Russian censors. (Shown, singer Chaliapin as Boris Godunov in Mussorgsky's opera based on Pushkin's tragedy.) Pushkin duels with his frivolous wife's lover; dies at age 38.

1834 Honoré de Balzac's novel *Le Père Goriot* (*Father Goriot*) tells of a father's devotion to his unworthy daughters. Prolific Balzac (seen in Rodin's famous statue) names his interlocking series (90 novels with 2,000 characters of all social classes and types, completed in less than 20 years) *The Human Comedy*. Although Balzac is considered founder of French Realism for his copious detail about lives of ordinary people, his plots are melodramatic, the characters often extreme, and the rhetoric windy. Oscar Wilde quips that Balzac invented 19th century with his seemingly objective documentation of French social history. (Balzac himself states he completes with his pen the conquest that Napoleon began with a sword.) Legendary for superhuman energy, appetite, and panoramic scope of ambition.

1835 Alexis de Tocqueville writes landmark study of American character and institutions in *De la démocratie en Amérique* (*Democracy in America*), a classic of political analysis. French historian identifies crucial factor of balance between self-rule and need to control unruly tendencies. First objective study of American principles in action, his observations on class structure, religion, and racism are remarkably penetrating. De Tocqueville seen in portrait by Theodore Chasseriau.

1836 Ralph Waldo Emerson's essay "Nature" defines transcendentalist philosophy. Emerson leaves his profession as Unitarian preacher, concluding, "to be a good minister it was necessary to leave the ministry." In public lectures, poems, and essays, he is chief oracle of transcendentalism in America. Urges self-reliant individualism and intuition as means to grasp divinity in nature and humanity. Inspiring epigrams express optimistic faith in human goodness and progress: "A man is a god in ruins. When men are innocent, life shall be longer, and shall pass into the immortal as gently as we awake from dreams."

American Renaissance

"We have listened too long to the courtly muses of Europe," Ralph Waldo Emerson proclaims in "The American Scholar," adding, "We will walk on our own feet; we will work with our own hands; we will speak our own minds," Answering this call to use local life and lore as a subject for art, American authors in the mid-19th century create a national literature of the highest order. Parallel to the proud, nationalist spirit fed by settling the Continent, a magnificent cultural flowering occurs. Infected by literary Romanticism, authors explore the gains and losses of America's penchant for individualism and rejection of tradition. Emerson, Thoreau, and Whitman share a belief in man's natural goodness, tutored by nature, while Edgar Allan Poe, Hawthorne, and Melville are skeptical about human nature and convinced of the inevitable taint of evil. No longer imitative and didactic, American literature comes into its own.

1836 Nikolai Gogol's comic play *The Inspector General* opens in Moscow. His novel *Dead Souls* (1842) is acclaimed as one of Russia's finest; most famous tale is "The Overcoat." At age 22 Gogol has 1st hit with humorous sketches about life in the provinces. His works develop from folkloric material to theatrical portrayal of Ukrainian life, but his imagery is evocative more than realistic. Gogol's expressionism makes him father of Russian Modernism. Prose narration, like conversation, meanders through digressions, is more concerned with the fantastic than the real, as in story "The Nose," where a character's nose disappears from his face and turns up "by himself" in the street.

1836–52 French Romantic poet and playwright Alfred de Musset writes *Poésies Nouvelles* (*New Poems*), including his best-known lyrics "Les Nuits." In "La Nuit de Mai," he writes: "The most despairing songs are the loveliest of all,/ I know immortal ones composed only of tears." Cleaving to formula of Byronic passion, his early verse wallows in ecstasy and desolation of love: "Doubt,if you will, the being who loves you, / Woman or dog, but never doubt love itself." Enslaved to champagne, opium, and loose women, Musset is delicately handsome and dissolute. His work turns darker, disillusioned ("I have come too late into a century too old.") after his lacerating love affair with George Sand.

1837 Scotsman Thomas Carlyle publishes 1st installment of his massive *History of the French Revolution*, rewritten after friend John Stuart Mill used 1st manuscript as kindling to start fire. It makes his reputation, and the critic/historian exerts great influence in Europe and America as social prophet, known for exclamatory, savage style called "Carlylese." His spiri-

tual autobiography, *Sartor Resartus* (*The Tailor Re-tailored*), contains, he admits, "more of my opinions on Art, Politics, Religion, Heaven, Earth, and Air, than all the things I have yet written." Known as "the Sage of Chelsea," Carlyle vehemently attacks materialism and hypocrisy, believes in power of the individual but puts trust in heroic leaders more than the masses. Seen in painting by Abbott McNeill Whistler.

1841 American author Edgar Allan Poe invents modern detective story with "Murders in the Rue Morgue," featuring his amateur sleuth Dupin, who solves crimes through "ratiocination." In 1839, Poe publishes his 1st collection of macabre short stories, *Tales of the Grotesque and Arabesque*. Poe is known for short stories replete with Gothic trappings that reflect a nightmare view of the world. In both his grotesque tales and dark poetry, characters are obsessed by fear of death. The strange horrors of his morbid tales contrast to his use of supreme logic in his detective stories. Shown, illustration for hallucinatory short story, "Fall of the House of Usher."

1838 Alphonse de Lamartine, 1st French Romantic poet, publishes *La Chute d'un ange* (*The Fall of an Angel*). Engraving from English newspaper shows the liberal Lamartine, leader in French provisional govern-

ment, addressing a crowd in Paris. A radical republican and orator influenced by German Romanticism, Lamartine breaks from ornate "Noble Style" tradition of French Neoclassic verse. Irregular lines and stanzas comprise a major change. New melancholy mood for new age is termed *mal du siècle*, a disillusioned world-weariness after the heights of the Napoleonic Empire.

> So love and let us love! Rejoice with speed
> In this short, passing hour!
> Man has no port, and time too has no shores;
> It flows, and we pass on.

Invention of the Detective Story

Poe's "Murders in the Rue Morgue" 1st introduces the figure of a hyperintelligent layman who collects clues to solve the mystery of a crime. Sir Arthur Conan Doyle furthers this paradigm with his sleuth Sherlock Holmes, who applies his brilliant powers of analysis and deduction. Popular fiction in the genre includes works by Agatha Christie, Ellery Queen, and Erle Stanley Gardner. In the U.S., a more realistic style of the "hard-boiled" detective 1st appears in "pulp" magazines featuring street-smart private eyes who're more clever and resourceful than brilliant. Tough-guy detectives—no strangers to violence—are created by Dashiell Hammett, Raymond Chandler, and James M. Cain.

1841 British Victorian poet Robert Browning publishes sentimental *Pippa Passes*, a play in verse set in Italy. Browning departs from confessional style and exhibitionism of Romantic poets by phrasing poems as dramatic monologues by imagined characters drawn from European and Mediterranean past. Attitude toward evil characters is detached, nonjudgmental, but he implies evil is rejection of life. He captures energetic striving of his time, as in "Fra Lippo

Lippi," using the Renaissance painter as his spokesman who concludes: "This world's no blot for us, / Nor blank; it means intensely, and means good." *The Ring and the Book* (1869) is Browning's masterwork, which concludes that justice prevails. Shown, Kate Greenaway's illustration for poem "The Pied Piper of Hamelin."

1845

1845 American feminist Margaret Fuller's *Woman in the Nineteenth Century* calls for equality between sexes. A journalist, lecturer, participant in the utopian community of Brook Farm, and noted transcendentalist writer of tracts, Fuller is a passionate, magnetic advocate of women's rights. Friends with leading intellectuals like Emerson, Thoreau, Hawthorne, Bronson Alcott, and Horace Greeley, who enjoy her spellbinding conversation and lucid arguments, Fuller devotes herself to causes like abolitionism, prison reform, and women's suffrage. As Emerson testifies, "She was an active, inspiring companion and correspondent, and all the art, the thought, the nobleness in New England seemed at the moment related to her and she to it." After fighting unsuccessfully for Italian independence, she dies in a shipwreck at age 40.

1847 Brontë sisters (shown in rectory, writing) publish Romantic, Gothic novels *Wuthering Heights* (by Emily Brontë), *Jane Eyre* (Charlotte Brontë), and *Agnes Grey* (Anne Brontë). *Jane Eyre* portrays an unconventional heroine with feisty, independent spirit, who attracts her employer, a grim Byronic hero named Rochester. The narrative vigor and emotional appeal of the story make the novel an immediate success. The lyric poetry and vivid descriptions of the moors in *Wuthering Heights* contribute to Emily's forceful, imaginative tale. ("Wuthering" is a Yorkshire

word that refers to turbulent weather, a thematic motif in the agitated world of the novel.) The story revolves around the fierce, brutal Heathcliff's quest for revenge, a tale of mystic intensity.

1847 William Makepeace Thackeray's *Vanity Fair* introduces upwardly mobile schemer Becky Sharp. Moralistic satire of British society traces fortunes of penniless orphan Becky, and Amelia Sedley, sheltered daughter of prosperous merchant. Although both girls attend same boarding school, they are unlike in character and aspirations. Becky's machinations temporarily make her shine in London society, while Amelia suffers virtuously. (Shown,

Thackeray's illustration for the last chapter, "Virtue Rewarded.") Sardonic style carries reader forward with observations like: "This I set down as a positive truth. A woman with fair opportunities and without a positive hump, may marry whom she likes" and "If a man's character is to be abused, say what you will, there's nobody like a relation to do the business."

1849 English critic John Ruskin revives interest in Gothic architecture with *The Seven Lamps of Architecture* and *The Stones of Venice* (1851–53), hoping to save

medieval buildings from neglect. In manifold writings on art and architecture, the immensely influential and persuasive writer maintains there's an indissoluble connection between the morality of an artist, nobility of his ideas, and greatness of the art. Gradually his art criticism becomes social criticism, as Ruskin concludes Gothic architecture is built on a pure national faith, virtue, and benevolent social conditions. Argues against competitive capitalism and for a return to feudal, Christian ideals. In 1871, he founds Utopian society, Guild of St. George, but toward end of his life, he suffers from emotional instability and fits of insanity.

1850 Elizabeth Barrett Browning publishes *Sonnets from the Portuguese*. Tender poems describe evolution of her love for poet Robert Browning, who becomes her husband. Most famous sonnet begins: "How do I love thee? Let me count the ways." During idyllic,

15-year marriage, the couple lives in Florence, Italy, where Elizabeth is passionately devoted to the cause of Italian liberty. Her masterwork is 11,000-line poem *Aurora Leigh*, "a novel in verse" telling life story of female writer. The poet, who has a history of respiratory ailments, dies in 1861.

1850

1850 Nathaniel Hawthorne writes "allegories of the heart," delving into frailties and aspirations of humanity in novel *The Scarlet Letter* and short stories like symbolic "The Minister's Black Veil" in *Twice-Told Tales* (1837). Hawthorne hailed by Melville as having "great power of blackness," is 1st to write American tragedy on conflicting demands of spirit and nature. Concerned with cor-

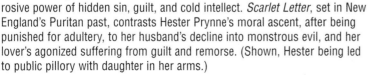

rosive power of hidden sin, guilt, and cold intellect. *Scarlet Letter*, set in New England's Puritan past, contrasts Hester Prynne's moral ascent, after being punished for adultery, to her husband's decline into monstrous evil, and her lover's agonized suffering from guilt and remorse. (Shown, Hester being led to public pillory with daughter in her arms.)

1850 English poet Dante Gabriel Rossetti writes "The Blessed Damozel" (shown, his painting to illustrate poem). Torn between painting and poetry, in both he glorifies ideal world of Arthurian legend, full of romantic color. An eminent Pre-Raphaelite painter, Rossetti uses similar techniques in poetry: sharp visual detail, medieval subjects, and an erotic, emotional tone.

In "Blessed Damozel," a beautiful lady with hair "yellow like ripe corn" leans out from "the gold bar of Heaven" praying for reunion with her earthly lover. Rossetti admires "grace and decorative charm" in art and embodies these qualities in his verse. He celebrates exotic trappings of chivalric age and possibility of purely Platonic love, such as his idol Dante felt for Beatrice. Poems translate his moods and experiences into symbolic, quasi-allegorical form.

Life at the Funny Farm

Rossetti's fondness for animals knows no bounds. Among his pets are hedgehogs, dormice, owls, rabbits, kangaroos, wombats, a wallaby, marmot, armadillo, raccoon, and various birds of all persuasions. He buys a Brahmin Bull because the beast's soft eyes remind him of his beloved Janey Morris, but it proves, as Evelyn Waugh recalls, "quite unmanageable." Needless to say, the denizens do not coexist seamlessly in his household and Rossetti greets their frequent demise with composure. Once, when walking with the poet W. B. Yeats's father, Rossetti notices a chaffinch, visibly upset, fluttering along the path beside him. Rossetti nods toward the bird, saying sadly, "That is my wife's soul." The finch immediately alights on his shoulder.

1854 In *Walden*, American transcendentalist Henry David Thoreau resolves to "simplify, simplify, simplify" his life at Walden Pond. He determines to

do without possessions, except for minimal necessities, in order to live fully. (Shown, his hut at Walden.) Thoreau inveighs against convention and champions those who forge their own path: "Only that day dawns to which we are awake. There is more day to dawn. The sun is but a morning star." Refusal to pay poll tax to support Mexican War inspires his 1849 essay "Civil Disobedience." Inspires Gandhi to liberate India from colonial rule and Martin Luther King Jr.'s philosophy of nonviolent opposition to injustice. On Thoreau's deathbed, aunt asks if he's made peace with God. Thoreau's answer: "I didn't know we'd ever quarreled."

1851 Herman Melville writes profound novel *Moby Dick* about obsessive quest of Captain Ahab to kill white whale, a metaphysical tragedy rich with symbolism. Melville, as his friend Hawthorne writes, could "neither believe nor be comfortable in his unbelief." Works like *Benito Cereno* and *Billy Budd* examine dichotomy between freedom and destiny, good and evil. Concern is not with man's social role but his ultimate fate. Indomitable Captain Ahab, an "ungodly," "god-like" man, refuses to accept human limitations. He defiantly asserts his individual will, even against the force of nature. Although Ahab's pride brings disaster, Melville admires his courage: "better is it to perish in that howling infinite, than be ingloriously dashed upon the lee, even if that were safety!"

1855 Walt Whitman's *Leaves of Grass* is 1st published; poet tinkers with book, adding poems until death in 1892. Called by Emerson "the most extraordinary piece of wit and wisdom that America has yet contributed," book still reigns as greatest poetry produced in U.S. Free verse approximates cadences of speech. Sprawling poems with radical rhythms are intensely emotional, gushing and explosive. He concludes "Song of Myself" with personal paean to reader: "I bequeath myself to the dirt to grow from the grass I love, / If you want me again look for me under your boot-soles. / … Failing to fetch me at 1st keep encouraged, / Missing me one place search another, / I stop somewhere waiting for you."

1855 Frederick Douglass, born as a slave on Maryland plantation, writes autobiographical *My Bondage and My Freedom*, example of fugitive slave narrative before Civil War. Exposes both atrocities of Southern slavery and

discrimination in North. In writings and oratory, Douglass offers persuasive evidence to combat prevalent myth that Africans are inferior, "knee-bending" race fit only for subservient, manual labor. His burning indignation and portrayal of cruelty and brutalization of slavery powerfully influence movement for equality.

1857 Charles Baudelaire's *Les Fleurs du Mal* (*Flowers of Evil*) kicks off vogue for morbid, grotesque imagery and French literary movement known as Symbolism. Influenced by Poe, he explores the macabre, lending new

psychological depth to poetry. He innovates not only in technique but subject of poetry. Poems address not nature but urban chaos. "The Carcass" describes repulsive reality of rot: "a vile carcass on a pebbly river bed, its legs in the air like a lustful woman, consumed and exuding poisons, exposed n careless, shameless fashion, its belly filled with effluvia." Poems include litanies to Satan; banned as obscene; prosecuted for blasphemy. Also an influential art critic, Baudelaire urges artists to be outrageous, to "shock the bourgeois," solid citizen.

1856 Gustave Flaubert publishes *Madame Bovary,* which takes 5 years to write. He's considered a Naturalistic writer for his precise observation, mass of details, objective tone, and meticulous word choice. He labors for hours over each sentence, struggling to find *le mot juste* (the one right word): "You don't know what it is to spend an entire day with one's head in one's hands, taxing one's poor brain in search of a word." Emma Bovary, an unhappily married housewife, thirsts greedily "for the warm breeze and scents of love" only to meet disappointment. (Shown, Emma Bovary's deathbed.) The widely quoted adage *"Madame Bovary c'est moi"* alludes to reader's intense identification with Emma's daydreams and pain.

French Symbolism

French post-Romantic poets, who are committed to pure, hyperaesthetic art, are called Symbolists. In the last 30 years of the 19th century, a group of poets, inspired by Baudelaire and Poe, revolt against the realistic novel with its minute, cold descriptions of mundane fact. They are also known as *Décadents* for their focus on sensational aspects of behavior like the perverse, morbid, and unconventional. Instead of describing external appearance, Paul Verlaine, Arthur Rimbaud, and Stéphane Mallarmé probe inner reality in poems that plumb the human psyche. They abandon photographic accuracy in order to invoke and imply through mysterious symbols. Continuing into another generation, in 1891 the poet Paul Valéry attends Mallarmé's Symbolist salons with the writer André Gide.

1860 Spanish post-Romantic poet Gustavo Adolfo Bécquer (seen in portrait painted by his brother, artist Valeriano Bécquer) publishes *Rimas* (*Rhymes*). One of most important Spanish poets, a founder of modern lyricism, he specializes in brief, musical poems on love. In a tone of melancholic longing, Bécquer examines love in all its facets: illusion, hope, joy, pain, and solitude. His poems are simple, sensitive, and expressive, without sentimentality: "What is poetry? You say while you nail / Your blue pupil into mine. / What is poetry? / And you ask me that? / Poetry . . . is you." Bécquer dies in 1870 an impoverished bohemian who at age 34 states, "While there is mystery for mankind, there will be poetry."

1862 Emily Dickinson sends 4 poems to an editor and is advised against publishing them. (Only 8 are published in her lifetime.) Considered eccentric by her Amherst, Massachusetts, neighbors who dub her "moth," the reclusive Dickinson dresses solely in white, rarely ventures from home. Only after her death in 1886 are 1,800 poems discovered. Her passionate, innovative verses deal with death, love, beauty, and nature. Her irregular rhythms, imperfect rhymes, and playful paradoxes are charged with intense feeling. The startlingly original metaphors yoke together finite, domestic details and speculations on the infinite. Her gnomic poetry fulfills her own mandate to "tell all the Truth but tell it slant— / Success in circuit lies."

1861 Charles Dickens, perhaps England's greatest novelist, creates immortal characters in masterpiece *Great Expectations*. The boy Pip, in love with Estella, must win over Estella's benefactor, crazed Miss Havisham (shown, in her tattered wedding dress). Dickens's 1st novel, *The Pickwick Papers*, is published when he's 24, the same time he serializes *Oliver Twist*, to instant popularity. Dickens's father goes to debtors' prison, and Dickens works at a blacking factory at age 12. Memories of the barbarous mistreatment of children, which he both suffers and observes, inform the autobiographical *David Copperfield*. His works combine rollicking humor, quirky characters, and social consciousness, indicting the abuse of the poor. He creates memorable characters that run the gamut of humanity, villains like Uriah Heep and the saintly, gentle blacksmith Joe Gargery.

1862 Ivan Turgenev, seen in self-portrait, publishes novel *Fathers and Sons* on conflict between Old World aristocracy who support serf system and populist intelligentsia fomenting democratic ideas. One of leading novelists and short story writers, he is 1st Russian writer well known outside his native land. Works concerned with social and political issues. Masterpiece *Fathers and Sons* flirts with nihilist and Materialist philosophy embodied in rebellious main character. Novel arouses extreme controversy, and embittered Turgenev spends most of life in France; advocates Westernization of Russia.

1865 Count Leo Tolstoy's monumental, realistic novel *War and Peace* makes him famous in Russia. Historical novel of panoramic scope contains more than 500 characters from all social classes. Centers on characters' search for meaning. Tragic tale of *Anna Karenina*

(1875) relates heroine's adultery and suicide (shown, Greta Garbo as Anna in 1935 film). Tolstoy presents mass of exact detail but rejects materialism, urging return to nature and instinctual life of essentials. Although born an aristocrat, in later years Tolstoy becomes a public figure who gives up wealth to live like a peasant. "With one hand I take thousands of rubles from the poor," Tolstoy writes, guilt-ridden over profiting from serfs' labor, "and with the other I hand back a few kopecks."

1865 Lewis Carroll publishes children's classic *Alice's Adventures in Wonderland*. Begun as an improvised story for young girl Alice Liddell and her sisters during boat trip, Carroll (pen name of Oxford mathematician C. L. Dodgson) expands tale and writes later sequel, *Through the Looking Glass*. Fantasy stories full of whimsy, nonsense, memorable scenes and characters. Alice falls down rabbit hole into land of topsy-turvy absurdity, presented without moralizing. After Alice plays mad croquet match using flamingo for mallet, Queen of Hearts (shown) yells, "Off with her head!"

Children's Literature

Following Rousseau's more humane theories of education, the 1st books appear specifically to entertain and instruct children. Fairy tales compiled by the brothers Grimm (1823) and stories by Hans Christian Andersen (1846) appeared earlier, but now a flood of fine fiction attracts juvenile readers. Louisa May Alcott's *Little Women* (1868) and Anna Sewell's horse story, *Black Beauty* (1877), illustrate the range of such books. In Beatrix Potter's *The Tale of Peter Rabbit* (1902) and A. A. Milne's *Winnie the Pooh* (1926), both text and pictures are equally important. Later standouts include British writers Frances Hodgson Burnett's *The Secret Garden* (1911) and J. R. R. Tolkien's fantasy *The Hobbit* (1937), as well as American Laura Ingalls Wilder's *Little House on the Prairie* series and the Canadian writer L. M. Montgomery's *Anne of Green Gables*.

1866 Paul Verlaine writes *Poèmes Saturniens* (*Saturnine Poems*). Later has disastrous love affair with protégé Arthur Rimbaud, which ends when Verlaine shoots and wounds the youth and is sentenced to 2 years in prison. (Shown, Verlaine at left and Rimbaud at right in painting by Fantin-Latour). Later poems impressionistically invoke shifting atmosphere, common sights, ephemeral feelings. Lives dissolute, bohemian lifestyle of alcoholism and poverty. Invents term *poète maudit* ("damned poet") to describe gifted poets like his fellow Symbolist Mallarmé who are mistrusted and maligned by society. From "Chanson d'Automne" ("Fall Song"): "The long sobs / Of the violins / Of autumn / Hurt my heart / With a monotonous / Languor."

1866 Russian novelist Fyodor Dostoyevsky publishes brilliant *Crime and Punishment*, tale of impoverished student Raskolnikov, who murders pawnbroker, suffers tormented conscience before earning redemption. *The Brothers Karamazov* (1880) is one of greatest modern novels, deals with religious, ethical, and social quandaries. His philosophy stresses

freedom of choice, worth of individual —even in a fallen state—human bond of love, need for repentance and compassion. "Believe me, that for the immense mass of mankind beauty is found in Sodom. Did you know that secret? The awful thing is that beauty is mysterious as well as terrible. God and the devil are fighting there, and the battlefield is the heart of man" (from *Brothers Karamazov*).

The Russian Novel

Although Nikolay Vasilyevich Gogol initiates Realistic prose with his tales of provincial life, their fantasy elements and dream sequences diverge from Realism. The Golden Age of fiction in Russia consists of masterpieces of Realism, tackling most subjects with a dark current of brooding introspection. Turgenev's novels criticize autocratic society, Dostoyevsky confronts the largest ethical issues, and Tolstoy examines the soul and society.

Ah, love, let us be true
To one another! for the world, which seems
To lie before us like a land of dreams,
So various, so beautiful, so new,
Hath really neither joy, nor love, nor light,
Nor certitude, nor peace, nor help for pain;
And we are here as on a darkling plain
Swept with confused alarms of struggle and flight,
Where ignorant armies clash by night.
—Matthew Arnold, "Dover Beach"

1866 British Aesthetic poet Algernon Swinburne's *Poems and Ballads: First Series* focuses on sensual love. Fevered poems horrify prudish Victorian society with incendiary call for political and sexual freedom. Intended to scandalize, his "Hymn to Prosperpine" denigrates Christ as lifeless "pale Galilean," predicting, "Yet thy kingdom shall pass, Galilean, thy dead shall go down to thee dead." In place of Christianity, Swinburne glorifies life of the senses, delights in the "noble and nude and antique." Influenced by Baudelaire, Swinburne attacks sermonizing trend in English poetry. Beautiful sounds and rhythm take precedence over imagery and ideas, which Swinburne calls "a tendency to the dulcet and luscious form of verbosity." Example: "Her gateways smoke with fume of flowers and fires, / With loves burnt out and unassuaged desires."

1867 Matthew Arnold's "Dover Beach" calls for love and truth, even as "sea of faith" ebbs in modern life. British Victorian poet strives mightily to make poetry an instrument of moral instruction, but personal depression intrudes. "Wandering between two worlds, one dead, / The other powerless to be born," he expresses sense of futility, loss, which is only alleviated by seeking solace in nature. Arnold wishes his poetry to be heroic, to "animate and ennoble" readers, even though its persistent tenor is melancholy. Goal is "to attain or approach perfection in the region of thought and feeling, and to unite this with perfection of form." "Dover Beach" blends frustration, fatigue, loneliness with desolation of an age of crumbling belief.

1871 George Eliot's moralistic novel *Middlemarch* features heroine Dorothea Brooke's attempts to live under social restrictions. An intelligent, idealistic young woman, Brooke longs to devote her life to a noble cause. She marries the aging, mean-spirited pedant Rev. Mr. Casaubon and is soon disillusioned.

Eliot, the pen name of Mary Anne Evans, freights her novels with reflection. Plots are vehicles for debate on social and ethical issues but also offer canvas on which to paint internal struggles. At age 9 Mary Anne sat alone at a children's party. When an adult asked if she was enjoying herself, the child gravely replied, "No I am not. I don't like to play with children. I like to talk to grown-up people."

1871 Precocious French Symbolist poet Arthur Rimbaud publishes *Le Bateau Ivre* (*The Drunken Boat*). While still in his teens, Rimbaud writes strikingly original poems, gives up literature before age 20. His life and letters alarm conservatives even more than his role model Baudelaire's. Raw images of poems are purposely offensive to conventional decency. Rimbaud flouts all taboos with poems on disgusting subjects like removing head lice. "Drunken Boat" records his liberation from tyranny of marketplace to seek experience in seething sea. Climaxes in cascade of hallucinatory images. Rimbaud cultivates Dionysian dementia in quest of revelation. Voice of extreme estrangement foreshadows Surrealism. Prose poem *Une Saison en enfer* (*A Season in Hell*, 1873) is tortured autobiography.

1875 English poet Gerard Manley Hopkins publishes "The Wreck of the *Deutschland*." Hopkins combines intense love for beauty of nature, fascination with (as he says in "Pied Beauty") "all things counter, original, spare, strange," and cultivation of his unique sensibility. He converts to Catholicism, becomes Jesuit priest in 1868, and writes no poetry for 7 years. When the ship *Deutschland* founders (illustration of shipwreck shown), he writes commemorative poem, which examines divine providence, justifying tragedy. Calls his offbeat metrical cadences "Sprung Rhythm." Aims for incantatory but natural effect like spoken song. Verse is compressed, terse, like checkmate in 3 moves.

Nothing is so beautiful as spring—
When weeds, in wheels, shoot long and
    lovely and lush,
Thrush's eggs look little low heavens, and thrush
Through the echoing timber does so rinse
    and wring
The ear, it strikes like lightnings to hear him sing.
          —Gerard Manley Hopkins

Victorian Literature

During the 1st half of the 60-year reign (1837–1901) of Queen Victoria, England experiences rapid industrialization, explosive growth in urban population and wealth, and the rise of a middle class. It's a time of prosperity, stability, and complacent optimism as England expands its empire worldwide. In this euphoric phase, sentiments of smug patriotism, earnest self-satisfaction, and puritanic correctness become associated with the word "Victorian." Poets like Tennyson assume the mantle of prophet and extoller of virtue, while Dickens exposes the plight of the poor in working-class novels like *Oliver Twist*, *Hard Times*, and *Great Expectations*. Struggles between the newly powerful middle class, working class, and the old aristocracy are a dominant theme of literature. During the last 30 years of the Victorian age, economic crisis, widespread poverty, and erosion of religious belief due to discoveries in science and the theory of evolution lead to disillusionment with conventional morality. In this time of insecurity and upheaval, writers like Matthew Arnold, John Ruskin, Thomas Hardy, Samuel Butler, Oscar Wilde, Joseph Conrad, and George Bernard Shaw question Victorian assumptions and values.

1876 Stéphane Mallarmé's *"L'après-midi d'un faune"* ("The Afternoon of a Faun") uses idiosyncratic syntax and elliptical phrases to develop single idea. Leading proponent of French Symbolism, Mallarmé (seen in portrait by Édouard Manet) hosts Tuesday evening sessions attended by avant-garde poets like Paul Valéry, where he formulates aesthetic theories. Believes poet should express transcendent world and evoke thoughts

through implication rather than explicit description. Wants poetry to be abstract as music. This poem inspires composition by Debussy.

1879 Henrik Ibsen's convention-shattering play *A Doll's House* opens door to women's liberation as heroine slams door, walks out on patronizing husband. (Shown, actress Alla Nazimova as Nora in 1922 film.) Norwegian playwright is known as father of modern drama because his plays jettison 19th-century rules and introduce concerns of contemporary life. Plays are character driven more than ingeniously plotted, with realistic psychological conflict. Later play *Hedda Gabler* (1890) features powerful woman who seizes control of her fate. Ibsen's realistic dramas are 1st "problem plays" dissecting strain and stress of ordinary life.

1880 Émile Zola's novel *Nana* stresses influence of nature, birth, and environment, presented in mind-numbing detail, on life of heroine, a prostitute. Before venturing to write a word of description, Zola takes research to ultimate extreme, compiles thick notebooks of facts on subjects like mining and the stock market to ensure accuracy. Zola (seen in Manet portrait) is leading French novelist of naturalism. He undertakes 22-year-long, 20-volume series of novels to portray social history of 1 family. Pays meticulous attention to details—often sordid—and scientific objectivity.

1881 Henry James's masterpiece, novel *The Portrait of a Lady*, explores American heiress Isabel Archer's mistaken choice of a husband and its aftermath. In his international novels like *The American* (1877) and *Daisy Miller* (1878), James (seen in portrait by John Singer Sargent) combines novel of manners with clash-of-cultures theme of an American abroad. Naïve, innocent Americans confront complexities of European civilization and

discover their innocence is actually destructive ignorance. His late style is long-winded, obscure, allusive, if not downright enigmatic. It forces reader to decipher not only details of plot but characters' perceptions and their psychological and moral states. Prolix style is an attempt, James says, to capture "the atmosphere of the mind."

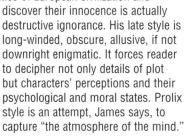

1881/1890 Anatole France's *Le Crime de Sylvestre Bonnard* (made into opera by Massenet) is his 1st successful novel. Prominent French literary figure (shown on his deathbed in 1924) is known for urbane criticism, poetry, and elegantly satirical fiction. Allusive, ironic tone characterized by cynical mockery and graceful, sophisticated style. "To accomplish great things, we must not only act but also dream, not only plan but also believe."

1883 Scottish author Robert Louis Stevenson publishes 1st full-length work of fiction, *Treasure Island*, followed by *The Strange Case of Dr. Jekyll and Mr. Hyde* (1886), both huge hits. Stevenson is chronic traveler and vivid personality who

records his adventures on the road in travel pieces before turning to novels. His wanderings in the South Seas make him legendary figure called "The Story Teller." Escapist, thrilling tales of swashbuckling antiheroes and romantic *Doppelgänger* (double) theme attract large audience. He refuses to take himself seriously as author, calling his historical novels "tushery." "Fiction is to grown men what play is to the child," he boasts, as if his craft is a lark. Shown, *Treasure Island* buccaneers in illustration by N. C. Wyeth.

1883–92 Friedrich Nietzsche elaborates secular myth of superman in *Thus Spake Zarathustra*. Nietzsche (seen in portrait by Edvard Munch) is known for pithy epigrams, puns, and polemical rage. Style is ingenious, full of fury even when his arguments are compelling and cogent. Nietzsche exults in shock value of full-frontal assault on Christian beliefs in *The Genealogy of Morals* (1887), alternating between brilliant debate and spurious reasoning. Nietzsche calls strident tone of his writing "my attempt to philosophize with a hammer." Aim is to demolish all idols: "This little book is a grand declaration of war." He pays to publish his most important books, now considered unequaled in German literature. At beginning of 1889, Nietzsche collapses into insanity.

1884 Mark Twain's *The Adventures of Huckleberry Finn* shows tragedy of slavery, as escaped slave Jim and runaway Huck float on raft down Mississippi River. Twain is initially known as a humor writer specializing in tall tales of frontier. *Huck Finn*, a growing-up story, which involves radical disillusionment, describes small-town life, is masterpiece of colloquial writing, combining idiomatic speech, local source material, and seemingly guileless descriptions. Balance of humor and truth, innocence and malevolence, romance and realism highlights mythic journey to heart of American character and its moral quandaries. Work seems simple, while harboring deeply disturbing complexity. "All modern American literature," according to Hemingway, "comes from one book by Mark Twain called *Huckleberry Finn* . . . the best book we've had."

1885 Walter Pater's *Marius the Epicurean*, set in ancient Rome, is fictional biography with personal overtones. English author is master of refined prose, an exquisite aesthete, parodied as Mr. Rose, who epitomizes Aesthetic (art for art's sake) movement. With Swinburne and Rossetti, Pater takes up Pre-Raphaelite cause. His critical nonfiction *Studies in the History of the Renaissance* (1873) ends with famous line, "To burn always with this hard gem-like flame, to maintain this ecstasy, is success in life." Oscar Wilde proclaims influential book "the holy writ of beauty." "Why should we be good, Mr. Pater?" a young student asks. "Because," he answers, "it is so beautiful."

Aesthetic Movement: Art for Art's Sake

Concerned with a quest for beauty in art without a wisp of moral or political purpose, the Aesthetic movement aims for perfect technical craft. In France, the Symbolist poets espouse this doctrine of *l'art pour l'art*, and in England in the 1880s, Walter Pater announces the be-all and end-all of literature and painting is purely "the desire of beauty, the love of art for art's sake." A reaction against Victorian crusaders who lard their works with messages of improvement or reproof, the Aesthetics seek to eliminate all instruction and sleeve-tugging content, arousing sensual delight instead of indignation.

1885 William Dean Howells's *The Rise of Silas Lapham* is a quasi-Realistic American novel about a newly rich entrepreneur and his crisis of conscience. Howells is both proponent and practitioner of realism as editor of *The Atlantic Monthly* magazine in Boston and a writer of fiction. Theme of his novels is the manners of the American middle class. Protagonist of *Silas Lapham* is heroic but with minor flaws. Howells, branded as timid exemplar of "genteel tradition," wishes to portray "smiling aspects of life," avoiding sordid excesses of sensuality and unkempt passion. Exposes new moral dilemmas linked to sudden amassing of great wealth.

1888 August Strindberg's *Miss Julie* portrays both sexual and class warfare in person of aristocratic woman who has affair with a footman. Swedish playwright

(seen in portrait by Edvard Munch) knows poverty intimately from his difficult childhood. He 1st writes Realistic-Naturalistic plays on conflict between the sexes. Later, showing signs of mental instability—his "inferno crisis" —he dabbles in Swedenborgian mysticism, alchemy, and the occult. After an emotional crisis brings him to brink of insanity, his plays become more symbolic and expressionistic, employing innovative visual effects. Writes haunting "dream plays," surrealistic visions of his inner life. Considered father of Expressionism in drama.

1891 Poet Paul Valéry attends Mallarmé's Symbolist salons with writer André Gide, is inspired to analyze creative process and write poems reflecting inner turmoil of competing desires. Later masterpiece

La Jeune Parque (begun 1913) is free-flowing dramatic monologue, which attempts to attain his ideal "crystal systems" of "pure poetry." Theme is battle: Apollonian reason and intellect vs. Dionysian, irrational passion and inspiration. "Science is only a collection of recipes that always succeed. All the rest is literature."

1889 German playwright Gerhart Hauptmann stages 1st play *Vor Sonnenaufgang* (*Before Dawn*). Influenced by Ibsen, the play treats alcoholism in grim, Naturalistic style. First performance arouses firestorm of controversy, marks beginning of Naturalism in German theater. Hauptmann's early plays noted for detailed realism. Instead of heroic or historical events, they explore ordinary situations (sometimes employing local dialect and working-class characters) without contrived plots and with no artificial or didactic dialogue, no monologues or asides to the audience. Once established as *meister* of German literature, Hauptmann (seen in portrait by Max Lieberman) experiments with plays that blend naturalistic style and symbolic elements.

1891 Thomas Hardy's tragedy *Tess of the D'Urbervilles* is novel of pastoral Wessex ruined by modern world. The milkmaid Tess's idyllic love affair with harp-playing Angel Clare in paradisiacal garden in English countryside sets stage for her sacrificial end on altar stone at Stonehenge. Hardy portrays natural setting to suggest "the deeper reality

underlying the scenic." Tess's betrayal mirrors doomed simplicity of rural values, corrupted by new industrial forces and modern world. "My aim," Hardy says, "is to intensify the expression of things," to make "visibly visible" "the heart and inner meaning." Purpose of his last novel, *Jude the Obscure*, is "to tell, without a mincing of words, of a deadly war waged between flesh and spirit; and to point the tragedy of unfulfilled aims."

1892 William Butler Yeats's "The Lake Isle of Innisfree," inspired by Wordsworth and Thoreau, concludes: "I will arise and go now, for always night and day / I hear lake water lapping with low sounds by the shore; / While I stand on the roadway, or on the pavements gray, / I hear it in the deep heart's core." Irish nationalist poet, seen in portrait by his father John Butler Yeats, creates national theater, writes plays based on Gaelic legends, becoming one of greatest 20th-century poets. Bases theory of historic and personal development on spiral ("gyre"), image of winding stair. "The Second Coming" is apocalyptic vision of history. In "Byzantium" and "Sailing to Byzantium" richness of culture, civilization, and art triumph over death and decay.

An aged man is but a paltry thing,
A tattered coat upon a stick, unless
Soul clap its hands and sing, and louder sing
For every tatter in its moral dress.
—W. B. Yeats

Outnumbered

At a curtain call after the premiere of his early play *Arms and the Man*, Shaw acknowledges the enthusiastic audience's *Bravos* with a bow. A single hiss rings out from the gallery. Shaw addresses the dissenter, "I quite agree with you, sir, but what can 2 do against so many?" W. B. Yeats, a witness of the event, notes, "And from that moment Bernard Shaw became the most formidable man in modern letters."

1894 Irish playwright George Bernard Shaw writes *Arms and the Man*. A progressive freethinker, strict vegetarian, teetotaler, and socialist, he supports women's rights, income equality, and communal ownership of property. More than 50 plays evince acerbic "Shavian wit"—dry, satirical dissection of manners of upper and middle classes. The dramatic conflict is not in romance (although ostensible subject is money, matrimony, and morals) but tension between beliefs and values. Plays are mental tour de force of literate dialogue, infused with social and ethical passion. The indefatigable and iconoclastic reformer is at work on a comedy when he drops dead at age 94 in 1950. Shown, Laurence Olivier and Vivien Leigh in production of *Caesar and Cleopatra*, Shaw's 1898 play.

Utopian Literature

The 1st half of the 19th century is an age of optimism and idealism. Utopian communal societies flourish, as do humanitarian, reform movements of all stripes. The legacy of 18th-century science and rationalism, combined with 19th-century romanticism and religious cults, predisposes thinkers to dream of ideal societies. During the 1800s, hundreds of agrarian religious and secular communities are founded. By the latter half of the century, writers publish thoughts on how these communities might work (or not). William Dean Howells's *A Traveler from Altruria* points out how far America is from Utopia, while Edward Bellamy, in *Looking Backward*, imagines what blessings technology, morality, and affluence will bring in 2000. In *Back to Methuselah*, George Bernard Shaw suggests a plan to eliminate death and injustice, Charlotte Perkins Gilman devises a feminist utopia in *Herland*, and William Morris sees work as a creative act in *News from Nowhere*, where happy artisans weave and make tasteful wallpaper. Samuel Butler's *Erewhon* satirizes the concept and H. G. Wells admits total perfection is not possible in *A Modern Utopia*.

1894 Rudyard Kipling's fanciful children's tale *The Jungle Book* (1902) and novel *Kim* (1901) win him permanent acclaim. (Shown, Kipling's illustration for "The Elephant's Child" from *Just So Stories*.) British author, born in Bombay, India, achieves spectacular celebrity in London for poems and stories of the Raj. As unofficial poet of the empire, he is lionized by British readers. Poems like "If" memorized and recited by generations of schoolchildren. ("If you can fill the unforgiving minute / With sixty seconds' worth of distance run / Yours is the Earth and everything that's in it, / And—what is more—you'll be a Man, my son!") He falls into disfavor with anti-imperialist intelligentsia for jingoism and taint of racism. In both prose and verse, Kipling captures colloquialism of speech and ballads.

1894 Rainer Maria Rilke's 1st book of poems in German, *Leben und Lieder* (*Life and Songs*) appears. Austro-Hungarian's 1st poems show brooding, introspective Romanticism. Wandering from 1 European country to another, living with wealthy, titled patrons, Rilke (seen on Austrian postage stamp) indulges in search for life's meaning. Concludes meaning is realized in power of poet's voice to conjure and convey experience. Sculptor Rodin (whom Rilke serves as secretary) teaches that art is more than spontaneous overflow of emotion but a means to refine and communicate an idea, feeling, experience, or object. His work becomes less subjective and more crafted, with brilliant precision. Masterpiece is *Duino Elegies* (1922), personal visions and laments in chiseled phrases and daring imagery.

RAINER MARIA RILKE 1875-1926

REPVBLIK ÖSTERREICH

A. PILCH   1976   R. TOTH

3 S

1895 Stephen Crane's novel *The Red Badge of Courage* depicts man as puny ant, without free will, trapped in bestial Civil War and undermined by fear. Crane opposes Romantic fiction, writes 1st Naturalistic novel in America,

Maggie, A Girl of the Streets (1893), which documents squalid slum life and portrays heroine as hopeless victim. Crane views man as insignificant in world of hostile or indifferent forces, using striking imagery in idiosyncratic poems, novels, and short stories like masterful "The Open Boat." Crane carries quote from Emerson in his pocket: "Congratulate yourselves if you have done something strange and extravagant and broken the monotony of a decorous age." His honest, unvarnished writing alienates genteel readers.

The Naturalistic Novel

In a reaction against Romantic escapism and influenced by Darwin and Marx, French writers like Alphonse Daudet and Zola develop the naturalistic novel. Zola postulates the theory of a detached narrator who portrays human beings as in an objective case study, documenting conditions that affect their lives in precise and voluminous detail. The subjects are generally from the lower class and their fates are not self-determined but controlled by larger forces of heredity and environment. American Naturalist writers include Stephen Crane, Jack London, Hamlin Garland, Frank Norris, Theodore Dreiser, and later, James T. Farrell.

1895 Quipmeister Oscar Wilde produces classic comedy, *The Importance of Being Earnest*. As a brilliant student at Oxford, Irish-born Wilde dresses like a popinjay and—with his long, flowing hair and clutching flowers—disdains sport. He proclaims himself a devotee of Walter Pater and the Aesthetic movement: "There is no such thing as a moral or an immoral book. Books are well written or badly written. That is all." His sly, dazzling repartee is far removed from natural speech in plays like *Lady Windermere's Fan* and *An*

Ideal Husband. A flamboyant man-about-town, he's known for witty epigrams: "We are all in the gutter, but some of us are looking at the stars." Wilde runs afoul of the law, is convicted for homosexuality and imprisoned.

The youth of America is their oldest tradition. It has been going on now for three hundred years.

The English country gentleman galloping after a fox—the unspeakable in full pursuit of the uneatable.

—Oscar Wilde,
A Woman of No Importance

1896 A. E. Housman's collection *A Shropshire Lad* contains lyrics on lost youth and love, like "To an Athlete Dying Young." Housman, a classical scholar, composes anguished verse after beloved friend leaves him to marry and live in India. Housman becomes Latin professor and publishes, at his own expense, collection of 63 nostalgic poems based on ballad form and set in imaginary "land of lost content." Simple, poignant poems—many addressed to, or spoken by, a soldier—express fleeting nature of youth and love. When book becomes popular during WWI, a publisher offers to produce the book and to pay royalties. "I want no royalties," Housman insists. "I am a professor of Latin." He uggests any profits be used to reduce price of book.

1896 Edwin Arlington Robinson self-publishes 1st volume of poetry, which includes "Luke Havergal" and "Richard Corey." Of a meditative and melancholy disposition, Robinson recalls how, at age 6, he spent several hours in a rocking chair questioning why he'd been born. Sees not brightness of life but blight. Poems draw dark portraits of New Englanders encountered growing up in Gardiner, Maine, expose corrosive effect of Puritan ethic and how small-town life can lead to small minds. Although mostly pessimistic, he finds virtue in stoical endurance: "There's a good deal to live for, but a man has to go through hell really to find it out." Tragic vision expressed in typical poem: "Miniver Cheevy, born too late, / Scratched his head and kept on thinking; / Miniver coughed, and called it fate, / And kept on drinking."

1896 Anton Chekhov's *The Seagull* (shown, 2006 production with Hattie Morahan and Ben Whishaw) flops in 1st production at St. Petersburg, is hit in 1898 second staging in Moscow. Russian playwright shows fading landed gentry after serfs are freed; presents stories realistically with detached, skeptical outlook. Theme is man's aloneness in universe and society. Presents "slice of life" on stage, succession of scenes without dramatic plot or message, more concerned with atmosphere and characters' musings. Other masterful plays are *Uncle Vanya*, *The Three Sisters*, and *The Cherry Orchard*. Chekhov is also noted short story writer, whose motto is: "Conciseness is the sister of talent."

1896 Sarah Orne Jewett's *The Country of the Pointed Firs* describes hardships and pleasures of life in rural Maine. Jewett, who as a child accompanied her physician father on his rounds, says, "The best of my education was received in my father's buggy and the places to which it carried me." Her stories and sketches portray Maine men and women, their customs, virtues, and suffering in villages and farms. Outstanding example of regional fiction.

1896 Alfred Jarry's *Ubu Roi*, shocking when 1st produced, influences later birth of Theater of the Absurd and Dada art movement. (Shown, Joan Miró's illustration for play.) French dramatist is famous mainly for this stylized burlesque, translated as *Ubu the King*. Play originates in adolescent farce written at age 15 poking fun at obnoxious, pompous teacher. Satire on bourgeois complacency uses obscene language, ridiculous posturing, grotesquely exaggerated physique. Contains nonsensical non-sequiturs like,

"Mother Ubu, you're very ugly today. Is it because we have company?" Jarry is infamous for his bizarre, debauched behavior and championing of hallucinations over reason.

1897 Edmond Rostand's play *Cyrano de Bergerac* opens in Paris, is popular hit. French playwright's comic and historical plays diverge from Naturalistic trend. (Shown, Henri Matisse's *Cyrano*.) Touching, witty Neo-Romantic drama includes dashing soldier-poet hero with large nose, who allows handsome but shallow rival to use his witty words to win beloved Roxane. The dying but irrepressibly eloquent Cyrano says these parting words to Roxane: "There is, in spite of you, something that I'm taking, this evening, . . . when I enter the house of God . . . and it is . . ." Roxane prods him as he fades from life, "It is?" His last words: "My panache!"

1898 Maxim Gorky (pen name means "the bitter one") publishes 2 volumes of stories and sketches. Gorky, an orphan who's on his own from age 9, is 1st great Russian writer to come from ranks of proletariat. Before becoming a writer, he was dishwasher, fisherman, baker, railroad man, and unemployed tramp. Realistic stories describe down-and-out life through wretched characters from dregs of society, whom Gorky terms "creatures that once were men." His most famous drama, *The Lower Depths* (1902), is set in seedy flophouse inhabited by derelicts. The play poses question of whether one should lose oneself in deluded dreams of better world or admit sordid truth and rely on own limited powers.

1899 American author Kate Chopin's novel *The Awakening* shocks genteel readers with its poetic depiction of a high-society woman in New Orleans who liberates herself from husband and family to pursue her own inclinations. The heroine's infidelity and adultery are presented as necessities to preserve her identity. She has no regrets, except insofar as her acts harm her children. Heroine chooses suicide rather than conformity to the narrow strictures of society. "The artist must possess the courageous soul that dares and defies."

From Naturalism to Magic Realism, Modernism to Postmodernism and Beyond: The 20th Century

The first formative event for literature in the twentieth century is the big bang of World War I. The absurdity of trench warfare, in which soldiers are ordered to race out like lemmings to face machine-gun fire, and the nationalistic power grabs after the war cause widespread revulsion and abandonment of any lingering idealism in Europe. The standards of preceding generations are seen as responsible for the debacle of war. A new concept of the world, stripped of beauty, faith, and reason, is embedded in literary consciousness by T. S. Eliot in 1922 with *The Waste Land*.

The common trait of literature is innovation, epitomized by James Joyce's revolutionary novel *Ulysses*, which views the world from inside characters' heads, with utmost honesty. Antiwar novels like Ernest Hemingway's *A Farewell to Arms* strike a new note, dispensing with patriotic rhetoric. Social satires like Sinclair Lewis's *Babbitt*, Aldous Huxley's *Brave New World*, and George Orwell's *Animal Farm* attack reigning ideologies. H. L. Mencken pens scathing polemics against vulgar American culture, inhabited by the hapless "booboisie."

Since the first half of the century encompasses not only the Russian Revolution, two world wars, the atomic bomb, and a host of inventions that revolutionize life, it's no wonder these upheavals usher in the modern era. A general atmosphere of disillusionment and disconnection from the past produces a need to experiment in all art forms. Literature emphasizes personal experience and subjective aims rather than fidelity to external reality.

Modernism brings a rejection of all rules and a reveling in originality for its own sake. Stream-of-consciousness novels, Theater of the Absurd plays, and nearly incomprehensible poems like Ezra Pound's *Cantos* are as challenging as the atonal music of Schoenberg and the Cubism of Pablo Picasso. With tradition in tatters, artists step into the breach to discover new forms. On the Continent, writers like Thomas Mann and Franz Kafka, with his weird, dreamlike novels, rely on Symbolism, rejecting the Naturalism that was popular at the turn of the century. In drama, Bertolt Brecht's Expressionist plays distort reality to badger the audience into new awareness, and Eugene O'Neill takes up the mantle of experimentation in his early plays.

The United States doesn't experience the pessimism of Europe after World War I, but instead plunges into the hedonism of the Jazz Age. In contrast, Prohibition's ban on liquor in 1920, a harbinger of Puritanic repression and provincialism, causes writers like Hemingway and Fitzgerald to flee to Europe, where they absorb the radical artistic currents. A popular song of the time is "How're you gonna keep 'em down on the farm after they're seen Paree?" Certainly in literature as in visual art, contact with the French avant-garde changes the face of American art.

The breakdown in social and ethical patterns fuels an epoch of bravura creativity in literature, as writers take risks to develop new forms and explore new content. As John Dos Passos put it, from Paris spread in every direction "a certain Esperanto of the arts that had 'modern' for its trademark."

Back in the United States, the advent of the Depression in 1929 causes writers like John Steinbeck and Clifford Odets to examine critically the capitalist system. In literature as in New Deal society and politics, it's an era of questioning, reform, and flux.

From 1950 to 2000, social turmoil continues. With thirty million civilians killed in World War II (more than military losses) and the devastation of the atomic bomb unleashed in 1945, it begins to seem as if man's scientific and technological prowess might have outstripped his moral and emotional growth. The Beat poets and novelists in the United States and Angry Young Men in England express disgust with the conservative status quo, and Existentialism colors literature in France. The thought dawns that uncontrolled industrial exploitation could threaten the sustainability of the ecosystem. Issues of social justice and increasing secularization of society also occupy writers. Authors John Cheever and John Updike express suburban alienation.

Revolutions in civil rights, the women's liberation movement, student uprisings of the 1960s and '70s, the anti–Vietnam War movement, the sexual revolution, and multiple assassinations of public figures undermine authority and stability. After the 1960s, idealism declines into a postmodern stance of cynicism and irony, except in Latin America,

where the Magic Realism of such politically committed authors as Gabriel García Márquez unabashedly injects extravagant flights of fantasy into description.

The 1990s seem to usher in a rebirth of hope after the Berlin Wall falls in 1989, and the Cold War thaws. East and West Germany reunify; democracy gains a foothold in the former USSR, culminating in the Russian Republic. Nelson Mandela is released from prison after twenty-six years, marking a new phase in South African race relations, and the European Union merges old enemies in economic partnership. The first genetically modified vegetables are produced, the first animal is cloned (Dolly, the sheep), and the Internet erases all boundaries, symbolizing an era of globalization.

Yet for all the information available instantly from all parts of the world, confusion and frustration are widespread in contemporary life, especially after the terrorist attacks in New York City, Madrid, and London in 2001, 2004, and 2005, respectively. Worldwide unease over the chaos caused by the invasion of Iraq, and disenchantment caused by the misinformation used to justify it, add to the jittery mood. Literature continues to dissect the forces tearing us apart and holding us together, through stories and poems that reflect the human condition.

As Robert Frost said of poetry, "It begins in delight . . . and ends in a clarification of life . . . a momentary stay against confusion." Literature of the last hundred years, for all its taboo-busting bravado, still seeks to delight the reader's head and heart, to provide clarification about meaning and significance in life, and possibly to make inroads against confusion.

1900 Theodore Dreiser's 1st novel, *Sister Carrie*, suppressed by publisher for frank portrayal of heroine's amorality and sexuality. When 1919 edition appears, it establishes Dreiser's reputation. American author (12th of 13 children) leaves impoverished family at age 15 for Chicago, becomes journalist. *Sister Carrie* recounts working-class girl's ascent to "tinsel and shine" of celebrity as her lover's fortunes decline. Dreiser's mature masterpiece, epitome of naturalism, is *An American Tragedy* (1925). Hero is more victim of circumstance and yearning for wealth than captain of his destiny.

The Write Stuff

A survey of 125 respected authors yields a Top 10 list of major writers' favorite books. The most admired works of literature, according to frequency of citation, are: Tolstoy's *Anna Karenina*, Flaubert's *Madame Bovary*, Tolstoy's *War and Peace*, Nabokov's *Lolita*, Mark Twain's *The Adventures of Huckleberry Finn*, Shakespeare's *Hamlet*, Fitzgerald's *The Great Gatsby*, Proust's *Remembrance of Things Past*, Chekhov's short stories, and George Eliot's *Middlemarch*.

1900

1900 Joseph Conrad publishes novel *Lord Jim*, rife with ethical ambiguity probed through multiple viewpoints. Polish-born Conrad goes to sea at age 17, later learns English and leaves to pilot steamboat up Congo River in 1890. Hellish trip is fictionalized in 1902 novel *Heart of Darkness*. Conrad uses ship and seafaring life as microcosm to explore moral themes like the need for—and peril of—human communion.

1900 Colette's *Claudine at School* is 1st of 5 novels in series. (Shown, poster for operetta based on novels.) Her husband locks her in room until she produces requisite number of pages; she publishes 1st novels under pseudonym Willy, continues on her own after 1904. Colette, a music-hall dancer and mime at Moulin Rouge, scandalizes Paris with her tales of demimonde, full of witty dialogue in intimate style. Love affairs, as well as onstage kiss with lesbian lover during performance, shock society. In later years, public scorn changes to acclaim and Colette is hailed as France's greatest female writer. Of almost 50 novels, *Gigi* most popular.

74

1901 Frank Norris's novel *The Octopus* shows ranchers' resistance to greedily expanding railroad lines. *The Pit* (1903) paints epic struggle centered on a strong-man who tries to corner the wheat market and is defeated by uncontrollable forces.

A proponent of naturalism, American author strives for dramatic stories of individuals overwhelmed by heredity, environment, and history. Fiction is means to discover truth, slicing through "tissues and wrappings of flesh, down deep into the red, living heart of things."

1902 Italian poet, novelist, political revolutionary, and playwright Gabriele d'Annunzio's medieval tragedy *Francesca da Rimini* stars his lover Eleonora Duse. Hailed for originality and voluptuous decadence of his writing, the play is censored as immoral and closes after 3-week run. D'Annunzio is daredevil fighter pilot who leads 9 biplanes to Vienna in famous 1918 700-mile round-trip flight to drop propaganda leaflets. Poem "Rain in the Pines," inspired by his half-naked rides on horseback in the rain, is memorized by every Italian school child. Shown, Leon Bakst's 1917 costume sketch for d'Annunzio's tragedy *Phaedra*.

1901 André Gide finishes novel *The Immoralist*. Subject is "the ego and its own: the flesh." Themes of homosexuality and pleasure-seeking cause scandal when 300 copies are published in 1902. Frankness of groundbreaking novel is both shocking and exhilarating; launches Gide's reputation as most daring writer. Protagonist decides to live without burden of God or values, seeks life of sensuality, hungry for new experiences and erotic conquests. Frenchman Gide calls book "a fruit full of bitter ash." He's vilified by public that is indignant at hero's pure hedonism devoid of propriety and rules. "Liberated" protagonist comes to dead end, admitting, "This useless freedom tortures me."

1902 Vicente Blasco Ibáñez publishes novel *Reeds and Mud* about peasant fishermen in his native Valencia. Early naturalistic novels like this one and *The Cabin* considered his best. Spanish author is ardent republican partisan. Founds controversial newspaper that's so notorious, he's brought to court, censored, shot, and almost killed (bullet is caught in clasp of his belt, saving his life). Shown, Ricardo Cortes and Greta Garbo in 1926 film *Torrent*, adaptation of his spy novel *Mare Nostrum*.

1903 Paul Laurence Dunbar writes lyrics for Broadway musical *In Dahomey*. Parents were former slaves; father escaped to Canada, returned to fight in Civil War. Dunbar is only black in Ohio high school, president of literary society and school newspaper editor, after which he becomes elevator operator. Self-publishes poems and, invited by abolitionist Frederick Douglass, reads poems on "Negro Day" at Chicago World's Fair in 1893. Ambition is "to interpret my own people through song and story, and to prove to the many that after all we are more human than African." Dies at age 33, internationally renowned "Negro writer." Protests lynching in poem "The Haunted Oak."

Paul Laurence
Dunbar

American poet

10 cents U.S. postage

We smile, but, O great Christ, our cries
To thee from tortured souls arise.
We sing, but oh, the clay is vile
Beneath our feet, and long the mile;
But let the world dream otherwise,
    We wear the mask.   —Paul Laurence Dunbar

1903 Samuel Butler's semi-autobiographical novel *The Way of All Flesh*, published 1 year posthumously, dissects 4 generations of family, exploring struggle against inherited traits and middle-class attitudes. English author's satirical utopian novel, *Erewhon* (1872, an anagram of "nowhere"), attacks contemporary morals, science, and religion.

1903 Jack London's *The Call of the Wild* (shown, the dog Buck, featured in novel) makes him rich. London claws his way out of dire poverty, working as oyster pirate in San Francisco Bay, seaman on voyage to Japan, and Klondike gold prospector before collection of stories, *The Son of the Wolf* (1900), launches career as writer. Preaches socialist revolution, builds yacht to sail around world, runs for mayor of Oakland while writing melodramatic best sellers. Spends money as fast as he makes it; dies of alcoholism at 40. Works split between Darwinian survival of fittest and ideal of social solidarity.

1903 W. E. B. Du Bois publishes *The Souls of Black Folk*. Du Bois attends Harvard, is 1st black American to gain PhD. "I believe foolishly perhaps, but sincerely, that I have something to say to the world." As editor of NAACP magazine *Crisis*, he speaks for civil rights and social justice; writes: "He would not bleach the Negro soul in a flood of white Americanism, for he knows that Negro blood has a message for the world. He simply wishes to make it possible for a man to be both a Negro and an American, without being cursed and spit upon."

1905 Novel *The House of Mirth* establishes high-society matron Edith Wharton as serious writer. Dramatizes inner workings of genteel upper class, with its stifling social conventions. *The Age of Innocence* (1920), her finest novel, is set in upper-class New York during 1870s; expresses conflict between drive for individual fulfillment and pressure to conform. Novels of manners expose moral quandaries related to marriage and divorce. At age 11, Wharton began 1st attempt at fiction with: "If only I had known you were going to call I should have tidied up the drawing-room." Her mother chilled the girl's creative ardor with the icy comment, "Drawing-rooms are always tidy."

1907 J. M. Synge's *The Playboy of the Western World* causes riots in Dublin because of its honesty and realism, offensive to many (shown, 1928 production with Sara Allgood and Arthur Shields). Synge, influenced by Yeats, is part of Celtic revival of Gaelic and Irish literature that started around 1889. The goal is to create national art to express Irish consciousness by reanimating old myths and legendary heroes. Synge uses racy, exuberant language

of peasants, "as fully flavored as a nut or apple," as if overheard through "a chink in the floor." Rich folk idiom rivals lyrical Elizabethan speech. Synge dies at 39, eulogized by Yeats as "passionate and simple like his heart."

1906 Upton Sinclair's muckraking novel *The Jungle* exposes unsanitary conditions in Chicago stockyards, spurs reform. (Shown, butchers at Swift meat-packing plant in Chicago, 1904.) Sinclair documents abuses through reporting converted into fiction, which provokes passage of Pure Food and Drug Act. Approach is realistic presentation of significant social problems with goal of political reform. American author, more propagandistic than imaginative, is narrowly defeated for governor of California; fails to achieve goal of socialistic state, although meat consumption declines. "I aimed at the public's heart, and by accident I hit it in the stomach."

Muckrakers

American authors aghast at the inequitable distribution of wealth in the late 19th century, as well as the money panics, rapacious robber barons, and growth of slums and poverty, express the Progressive Era's call for reform. H. D. Lloyd's *Wealth Against Commonwealth* (1894) argues for social justice and reform. Thorstein Veblen, Jacob Riis (*How the Other Half Lives*), Ida Tarbell, Lincoln Steffens, Jack London, Upton Sinclair, and Gustavus Myers (*History of the Great American Fortunes*) join the protest movement in exposés of social ills. Muckraking reaches a peak in the 1st decade of the 20th century with mass magazines like *McClure's*, drawing public attention to corruption in business and politics.

1912 A passionate feminist and suffragette, Mary Austin rises above regional realism in novel *A Woman of Genius* with its strong, complex

female characters and depiction of trials facing a talented woman in a provincial town. In 27 books and more than 250 articles, Austin explores Native American and Hispanic traditions of the Southwest and argues for women's rights. In *Earth Horizon* she offers words of advice: "There was something you could do about unsatisfactory conditions besides being heroic or martyr to them, something more satisfactory than enduring or complaining, and that was getting out to hunt for the remedy."

1912 Austrian playwright Arthur Schnitzler's satirical comedy *Professor Bernhardi* is per-formed; critiques anti-Semitism. Early play *Anatol* (1893), about bourgeois playboy, is full of carefree Viennese wit, with amoral attitude toward sexuality. A physician who studied psychiatry, he probes psyche of characters in plays and novels, experiments stylistically. Eroticized writing considered immoral. His works are subject of obscenity

trials, and Schnitzler gains reputation as writer of pornography; perform-ances cause riots. In admiring letter, Freud pays tribute: "You have learned through intuition—though actually as a result of serious introspection—everything that I have had to unearth by laborious work on other persons."

1913 Marcel Proust begins 7-part *Remembrance of Things Past* with novel *Swann's Way*. He chronicles, over decades, fashionable social world: from luminaries to lower echelon of servants, panderers, and reprobates. Prevailing tone is of evanescence of life and affections. Central character of narrator unifies tales of dissolution. Long, leisurely sentences unfurl like

train of association inspired by involuntary memories. Famous madeleine cookie, for example, is like thread leading through the labyrinth of past joys. Proust, an asthmatic invalid, shuts himself up in cork-lined room, windows clamped shut, to write in bed. After making final changes to death scene in book, Proust dies of septicemia.

1913 D. H. Lawrence publishes *Sons and Lovers*, autobiographical novel, in which hero pursues sex with confusion and pas-sion. Lawrence expresses struggles of flesh as source of both fulfillment and frustration. Obsessive theme is limbo between lust and love. Intense pitch of novel *Women in Love* (1921) shows fear and fascination of sex. Four books suppressed, including *Lady Chatterley's Lover*, banned for obscenity. Even exhibition of his paintings is raided. Called "the novelist of the over- and the undersexed," his style is savagely honest, consciously barbaric and fierce. Sees world as rotten, perverted, and infected with malaise. Preaches gospel of virility as means for overcivilized man to regain potency, overcome Victorian hypocrisy.

1913 Spanish philosopher/playwright/poet Miguel de Unamuno publishes *The Tragic Sense of Life*. In philosophical writings that anticipate Existentialism, Unamuno examines conflict of religion and science, reason and belief; explores 20th-century materialism, man's solitude, and the absurdity of life. Novels concerned with abstract concepts more than individual characters and their actions. Aim is regeneration of Spanish culture through rediscovery of lost values, education, and opposition to provincialism. Personal creed: "My religion is to seek for truth in life and for life in truth, even knowing that I shall not find them while I live."

Imagism

Imagism makes the 1st break with conventional, petrified poetic forms and sentimentality. This school of "new" poetry originates in England and the U.S. around 1912 with Ezra Pound and T. E. Hulme. Promoted in *Poetry: A Magazine of Verse*, Imagists like Amy Lowell, William Carlos Williams, and H. D. (Hilda Doolittle) strip poetry of affected rhetoric and precious diction, substituting vivid, visual perceptions. Their creed is "to use the language of common speech, but to employ always the **exact** word, not the merely decorative word." Their motto: "conversation is the very essence of poetry." Conservatives denounce these principles as "heresies" and condemn the Imagists' free verse and unorthodox choice of subject. Typical works are short, observational poems with strikingly original metaphors. The movement dies around 1918, but its lasting influence liberates poetry from artificiality and encourages experimental form.

1914 New Englander Amy Lowell writes pictorial Imagist poems in free verse, as in collection *Sword Blades and Poppy Seed*. She becomes strident leader of movement, causing Ezra Pound to complain she converts Imagism into "Amy-gism." Known for her poetry readings, bevy of canine pals, habit of smoking cigars, and bold, sensual language, Lowell is public personality. Poem "Lilacs" is apostrophe to common flower: "Standing beside clean doorways, / Friendly to a house-cat and a pair of spectacles, / Making poetry out of a bit of moonlight / And a hundred or two sharp blossoms."

1914 Conrad Aiken publishes 1st volume of poetry, *Earth Triumphant and Other Tales in Verse*. Intense interest in psychoanalysis and identity is evident in musical, introspective poetry salted with puns and word play. American poet's verse is sensuous, with emphasis on sound of rising and falling syllables. Self-analysis of poetry flows like stream of consciousness.

1914 Poems in Robert Frost's *North of Boston* precisely observe hard, stony soil of New Hampshire and imply truths about dark struggle of life. New England poet milks cows at midnight and writes poems all night. First book hailed by Ezra Pound as "vurry Amur'k'n." Rejecting Modernist experiments, Frost sticks to "the old-fashioned way to be new," uses laconic Yankee speech and blank verse in both lyric and narrative verse. Seamus Heaney praises "his farmer's accuracy and his wily down-to-earthness."

Nature and chores like mowing, mending a wall, apple-picking are springboard for profound thought: "I'm always saying something that's just at the edge of something more." His credo: "A poem begins in delight and ends in wisdom."

1915 Czech writer Franz Kafka's short story "The Metamorphosis" tells of Gregor Samsa, turned into a gigantic insect. Son suffers disapproval of family and society

because of his difference. Matter-of-fact account of degradation and dehumanizing effect of being social outcast. Kafka's narratives report curious, improbable events and nightmarish fears. Rebellion, guilt, transformation, and repentance color tales, as does his sense of identity as a Jew, archetype of rootless, alienated Western man. Jean-Paul Sartre links Kafka's ambiguity to "the impossibility of transcendence"; alludes to his tendency to glimpse ever-receding reality as an evaporating mirage.

World War I Poets

The "war to end all wars," touted in the jingoistic press as "the great adventure," soon sours. Soldiers sign up by the thousands but find it's what one calls "the Late, Great Nightmare." Poets like Wilfred Owen, Charles Hamilton Sorley, and Robert Graves express bitter revulsion as they view horror at close range. As Realism replaces Idealism, their repressed emotions burst out in searing poetry "where," as Seamus Heaney says, "New Testament sensibility suffers and absorbs the shock of the new century's barbarism." Instead of celebrating noble heroism, they show tragedy. "The poetry is in the pity," Owen writes in a preface to poems he doesn't live to see published. One in 3 of these poets' schoolmates die in the war. "Red lips are not so red / As the stained stones kissed by the English dead."

1915 Rupert Brooke's WWI poems published posthumously in *1914 and Other Poems*. Handsome, 6-foot-tall, called "a golden

young Apollo," Brooke extends conversational tone in poems; enlists in war seeking to invigorate himself in struggle. Most promising of younger poets, he tames emotion into imaginative, intellectual gems, delights in life of the mind, senses, and feelings. Dies in 1915 at age 28, part of ill-fated Aegean Campaign. Poem "The Soldier" pleads, "If I should die, think only this of me; / That there's some corner of a foreign field / That is for ever England."

1916 In Carl Sandburg's *Chicago Poems*, guitar-playing crooner of folk ballads grabs Whitman's mantle as poet of democracy. American poet, seen in photo by his brother-in-law Edward Steichen, celebrates burly dynamism of American city. Poems capture vitality and strength of America during period of rapid growth, exult in patriotic fervor with swaggering verbosity, as in "Chicago": "Hog Butcher for the World, / Tool Maker, Stacker of Wheat, Player with Railroads and the Nation's Freight Handler; / Stormy, husky, brawling, / City of the Big Shoulders. . . ."

1912 Sherwood Anderson's short stories about Midwestern town are published in *Winesburg, Ohio*. Portrays "the ugliness of life, the strange beauty of life," with emphasis on thwarted hopes of provincials. American author's masterpiece is based on lonely

"grotesque" characters he knew as youth growing up, inarticulate individuals who yearn for communication but are doomed to fail. Tales told in realistic, simple style. Anderson gives form to characters' groping aspirations and secret needs. Obsessive theme is loneliness, alienation, yearning for contact. Caricature shows Anderson "wondering if . . . he is a greater realist than Zola."

1918 Willa Cather's novel *My Antonia* is epic vision of heroic daughter of immigrant family, infused with nostalgia for vanished past. Portrays pioneers' endurance and courage on Nebraska prairie. With what she calls "gift of sympathy," American author dramatizes lives of

simple settlers who struggle against obstacles and harsh environment to find meaning and embody nobility of self-reliant age. Typical subject is heroism of older, agrarian Midwest and decline during present industrial age.

1920 Sinclair Lewis publishes indictment of small-town life known as "revolt from the village" in *Main Street*, "where dullness is made God." Heroes of his novels oppose middle-class conventionality, rebel against conformity, and flee stultifying environment only to return in defeat. American writer grows up in small Minnesota town described in best seller *Main Street*,

novel that is both violently attacked and heatedly acclaimed for portrait of drab life devoid of culture. *Babbitt* (1922) has similar theme of impulse to freedom short-circuited by pressure to conform. Lewis is 1st American to win Nobel Prize for Literature in 1930, signal that American fiction has come of age on world stage.

1920

1921 Luigi Pirandello's *Six Characters in Search of an Author* performed. Italian playwright creates own genre of theater with startling innovations. Makes no attempt at credibility but peppers plays with implausible events and reversals. Incoherence of plays mirrors farcical reality and lack of faith in mankind. *Six Characters* is fiasco where embryonic "characters" invade stage rehearsal, demand that actors incarnate them, and are disappointed in results. Pirandello typically shows disparity between appearance and reality through perversely comic mockery.

1922 James Joyce publishes *Ulysses*, groundbreaking Modernist novel, banned in England and U.S. until 1933. As young man, Joyce rebels against Catholic upbringing and middle-class philistinism, chooses exile on the Continent, where he writes about Irish life from an emotional distance. His

subject is always Dublin but with application to all history, mythology, and human experience. *A Portrait of the Artist as a Young Man* (1916) fictionalizes Joyce's journey from rejecting tradition to embracing art. *Ulysses* narrates one day in the life of Everyman Leopold Bloom, with parallels to Homer's *Odyssey*. Book captures Bloom's subconscious mind in kaleidoscopic style that leaps between past and present, realistic description and inner monologue of multiple characters.

1922 T. S. Eliot paints picture of modern civilization in ruins in 40-page poem *The Waste Land*. Uses flashbacks, banal chatter, broken phrases, grab

bag of quotations from esoteric sources, and allusions to mythology to contrast past beauty to degraded present. Some call poem "filthy bedlam raving"; others, "greatest document of our day." Title describes disillusioned era—without purpose, beliefs, values—after the Great War. Leaping from one image to another, juxtaposing bits of lyricism and triviality, poem is like free-associated inner monologue. As in "The Hollow Men," Eliot portrays sterile life: "We are the hollow men," whose dried voices are meaningless as "rats' feet over broken glass." Famous conclusion: "This is the way the world ends / Not with a bang but a whimper."

In the American Grain: Regional Poets

In the early decades of the 20th century, native poets contrast to Modernists—erudite expatriates like Pound and Eliot—who derive their inspiration more from literature and mythology than local color. Poets like E. A. Robinson, Sandburg, and Frost treat the American scene and character, from New England farms to the big city, as their subjects. The regional poets use local idioms and speech patterns in verses dependent on poetic traditions established by their predecessors. Edgar Lee Masters's *Spoon River Anthology* (1915) pictures a complex roster of small-town characters. Troubadour Vachel Lindsay chants his poems, with percussion accompaniment, at the rousing pace of evangelical hymns. Robinson Jeffers in *Tamar and Other Poems* (1924) sets his misanthropic poems in California.

1923 E. E. Cummings's 1st volume of poems published in *Tulips and Chimneys*. A committed experimentalist, Cummings expresses romantic subjects through capricious typography, odd format, eccentric spellings, and scrambled grammar. A contrarian in life as well as art, American avant-garde poet lives without electricity, despises modern inventions like radio and television, condemns packaged food as "Battle Creek seaweed."

Indefatigably praises old-fashioned values like family bonds, fun, nature, intuition, love. Distrusts science and technology and believes rationality overpowers emotions to detriment of mankind. Lyrical, zesty poems celebrate simple subjects like springtime and joy in colloquial dialect—frank, occasionally bawdy, and playful.

1924 E. M. Forster's last novel, *A Passage to India*, shows clash of cultures, misunderstanding, and prejudice under the British Raj in colonial India. Novel shows injustices; expresses liberal humanism. Earlier work illustrates his maxim "only connect." Central aim is for individuals to unite "the prose with the passion" inside themselves.

Forster (seen in Dora Carrington's portrait) believes English middle and upper classes stifle spontaneous bursts of passion, intuition, and imagination. Urges that practicality and rationality be invigorated with sensitivity to nature and enjoyment of immediate experience, qualities he attributes to southern Europe and lower classes.

1924 Chilean Pablo Neruda publishes *Twenty Love Songs and a Song of Despair*. Surreal poems portray world of chaos and anguish. As an avowed Communist, Neruda becomes polemical populist poet, dies 12 days after Marxist president Salvador Allende is assassinated. Although dictator Augusto Pinochet denies permission for Neruda's funeral to become a public occasion, thousands of despondent fans use the funeral to stage the 1st protest against military strongman. Gabriel García Márquez calls Neruda "the greatest poet of the 20th century in any language."

1924 Thomas Mann's panoramic novel *The Magic Mountain* published. Erudite Mann is acutely aware that extreme sophistication may entail effete paralysis. Deals with conflict between coarse vitality and enjoyment and enervated aesthetic sensibility in *Death in Venice* (1913), where he links love of beauty to perversion and death.

1924 *Some Do Not*, Ford Madox Ford's 1st novel in WWI quartet *Parade's End*, is study of marital relations and wartime adventures of member of British ruling class. Tetralogy shows dismal changes after tragic war, including disintegration of society, morality, family, and hero's sanity. In idiosyncratic, Impressionistic language, describes fracturing of Old World and need for new code. Shown, 1923 photo taken in Ezra Pound's studio in Paris (left to right): James Joyce, Ezra Pound, Ford Madox Ford, and their patron, John Quinn.

1925

1926 Jean Cocteau adapts myth of Orpheus and Eurydice in play *Orphée*. French writer and director is at forefront of avant-garde in 1st half of 20th century, producing work in multiple genres, from ceramics and murals to music, ballet, and poetry. Constant theme is the poet-angel who guards man's divinity and defies fate. Famous film is surrealistic *Beauty and the Beast* (1945).

1925 Countee Cullen's 1st book of poems, *Color*, published when he graduates from New York University with a Phi Beta Kappa key. Other collections *Copper Sun*

and *The Ballad of the Brown Girl* make him star of Harlem Renaissance, but he gives up poetry; spends rest of life teaching in New York City public schools, occasionally collaborating on Broadway musicals. In "From the Dark Tower," writes, "We shall not always plant while others reap / The golden increment of bursting fruit, / . . . Not always bend to some more subtle brute; / We were not made eternally to weep / . . . So in the dark we hide the heart that bleeds, / And wait, and tend our agonizing seeds."

The Harlem Renaissance

In the 1920s and early '30s writers, artists, and musicians shine a new light on African-American culture. Centered in New York's Harlem, the 1st cluster of writers showing black life from an insider's perspective includes James Weldon Johnson, Claude McKay, Countee Cullen, Zora Neale Hurston, Jean Toomer, and Langston Hughes. Hughes, called the "poet laureate of Harlem," incorporates the rhythms of jazz and the blues in his poetry, using idiomatic language to great effect, as in "Mother to Son": "Well, son, I'll tell you: / Life for me ain't been no crystal stair. / It's had tacks in it, / And splinters, / And boards torn up, / And places with no carpet on the floor— / Bare. / But all the time / I'se been a-climbin' on."

The GREAT GATSBY

F·SCOTT·FITZGERALD

1925 In F. Scott Fitzgerald's best novel, *The Great Gatsby*, American author captures hollowness of dream of wealth and romantic longing for love in world with "all Gods dead, all wars fought, all faiths in man shaken." Fitzgerald chronicles (and epitomizes) Jazz Age glitter. Life during Roaring '20s for Scott and wife, Zelda, a perpetual cocktail party, as he squanders talent in debauchery. Describes Gatsby's mythic theme as "the loss of those illusions that give such color to the world that you don't care whether things are true or false so long as they partake of the magical glory." His typical characters are both beautiful, golden creatures and damned to moral ruin.

1925 American poet Ezra Pound's immensely long *The Cantos* reflect his knowledge and translations of poetry of all ages in many languages, including Latin, Old English, Old Provençal, Japanese, and Chinese. Influential poems are chaotic, like "a rag-bag to stuff all its thoughts in," or a repository where "I dump my catch, shiny and

silvery / As fresh sardines slapping and slipping on the marginal cobbles" (from *Canto II*). Pound shown in portrait by Wyndham Lewis.

1925 Ellen Glasgow's novel *Barren Ground* appears. Southern regional novelist and advocate of women's suffrage analyzes rapidly changing social conditions and their effect on women's lives. Writing from

Richmond, Virginia, Glasgow gives voice to dry comedy of manners and ironic view of civilized society, advocates stoicism in face of defeat.

1926 Sean O'Casey's antiwar play *The Plough and the Stars,* set during the Irish Easter Rising in 1916, considered insufficiently nationalistic, causes riots in Dublin when performed. Tragicomedies deal with Irish slum life, dangers and deceptions of revolutionary patriotism, national illusions. In rich, vigorous language, O'Casey dramatizes social conscience and political upheaval during Irish Civil War. Title for *Plough* derives from flag of Irish Citizen Army.

1926 Ernest Hemingway captures disillusioned postwar mood in *The Sun Also Rises*, agreeing with Gertrude Stein's comment, "You are all a lost generation." Shown, Hemingway at left with Lady Duff Twysden (model for Brett Ashley in novel) and his wife Hadley at Pamplona, where novel is set. American author employs terse style and monosyllabic vocabulary to filter out obsolete values, abstractions (meaningless "big words"), and certainty vanished from modern world. Novels *A*

Farewell to Arms (1929) and *For Whom the Bell Tolls* (1940) are masterpieces of economy and understatement. Classic hero exhibits "grace under pressure" to overcome fear.

1927 Virginia Woolf masters stream-of-consciousness style in *To the Lighthouse*. Finely crafted writing portrays truths about human experience through mimicking workings of human mind. Prose style

flows with rhythms and imagery of poetry, encompasses both action and introspection, external and internal events. Themes are the search for personal identity—especially women's quest for fulfillment—and the complexity of human relationships.

The Lost Generation

After the atrocities and horrendous loss of life of WWI, artists like Stephen Spender, Hemingway, and Fitzgerald feel the old absolute verities no longer apply. The war made them live from day to day and explore big themes of love, death, and responsibility. From 1920–30, young writers work in a period without stability or secure belief. Their writings reflect doubt and disenchantment. Called the "literature of nerves," these works revolt against the dead hand of the past in both form and content. Gertrude Stein ruptures conventions of the English language, using words for their tonal, abstract value. Joyce shatters and reinvents words, and E. E. Cummings declares, "To create is 1st of all to destroy" the old tricks of art, substituting "purely personal feeling. Which minute bit is art."

1929 French playwright Marcel Pagnol's *Marius* is 1st of sentimental trilogy about life in Marseilles. Shows lives of ordinary people and local scene captured in slang and dialect. Writes screenplays based on his plays and memoirs of his childhood in Provence. He's so revered for his work, he's 1st screenwriter/film director to be elected to the prestigious Académie Française. Shown, Fernand Charpin in 1931 film *Marius*.

1929 Austrian Franz Werfel's *The Pure in Heart* appears. This novel and *The Song of Bernadette* (1941) express yearning for brotherhood of mankind, but in 1938, Jewish writer flees Nazis and Austria. Novel *The Forty Days of Musa Dagh* (1933) is fictionalized account of 1915 massacre of Armenians by Turks.

1930 John Dos Passos publishes *The Forty-second Parallel*, 1st in *U.S.A.* trilogy. American author calls himself "red, radical, and revolutionary" (although he becomes quite conservative in later years). Novels attack corrupt capitalist system and Big Government, support underdog and workers, the oppressed and the poor. He lays bare rift between haves and have-nots. *U.S.A.*, through montage of narrative techniques, portrays vast social and political forces, showing disillusion after WWI and the little guy against "the Leviathan State."

1929 William Faulkner publishes masterpiece *The Sound and the Fury*. In 1950 Nobel Prize speech, Faulkner states theme: "the problems of the human heart in conflict with itself." Writes about fictional Yoknapatawpha County in Mississippi after discovering "my own little postage stamp of native soil was worth writing about and that I would never live long enough to exhaust it." Experimental techniques like fracturing time, narrative, and point of view and stream-of-consciousness monologues make works challenging. Considered by some the finest U.S. fiction writer ever, he examines burden of past on present, families that both strangle and strengthen, and fissures developing in close, conservative society. Panoramic scope of multigenerational sagas portrays Old South as boiling over with racial and class conflict.

The South Shall Rise Again

When an older culture is threatened by forces of change and people become aware of traditions slipping away, a surge of creative energy is often unleashed. Beginning in the 1920s and '30s, a Southern literary renaissance analyzes local customs and values, quite separate from the urbanized, industrial mainstream. The South proves fertile ground for authors like Faulkner, Ellen Glasgow, Erskine Caldwell, Eudora Welty, Caroline Gordon, Thomas Wolfe, Katherine Anne Porter, Flannery O'Connor, Carson McCullers, Tennessee Williams, Harper Lee, and Truman Capote. Contradictions rife in the South—guilt over slavery and racial discrimination, the divergence of Southern culture from the rest of America, and the conflict between a rural, traditional, religious society and modern secularism—give rise to significant, dramatic literature.

1930 Hart Crane intends his overwrought epic poem *The Bridge* as rebuttal to pessimism of T. S. Eliot's *The Waste Land*. Crane says aim is "a more positive" or "ecstatic goal." Uses Brooklyn Bridge as symbol of connection to express "feelings of elation . . . like being carried forward and upward simultaneously." Self-conscious attempt to create new American myth reflects Crane's refusal to accept that traditional values are in tatters. Doomed by chaos of personal life, he folds jacket over rail, leaps off ship into Caribbean, and swims out of sight. Hope for ecstatic national epic dies with him.

1931 Irish writer Frank O'Connor publishes *Guests of the Nation*, collection of short stories. With humor, sensitivity, and poetic language, he paints realistic pictures of Irish life. Presents full view of middle and lower classes, especially of "warm dim odorous feckless evasive southern quality" of life in his native County Cork.

1931 Edna St. Vincent Millay publishes 52 love sonnets in *Fatal Interview*. Strikes characteristic note of personal lyricism and passion. Considered a female Byron in early 1920s, popular poet portrays intense hunger for beauty, articulates ecstatic experience, laments loss of youth and descent of "the sun that will not rise again." Expresses despair over lost love: "And in my heart there stirs a quiet pain / For unremembered lads that not again / Will turn to me at midnight with a cry."

1932 Aldous Huxley's most popular work, *Brave New World*, is dystopian novel foreshadowing threats of misused science. Grim novel of ideas imagines world where scientific progress outstrips man's ethical development, warns of dangers of collective conditioning and passivity. Ironic title is at odds with futuristic world where embryos are produced in hatchery and consumers are bombarded with slogans for conformity. Individual, self-educated "savage" (who is outside control of World State and believes in moral choice) goes mad, commits suicide. In later years Huxley converts to mysticism, experiments with hallucinogenic drugs.

Modernism

Modernism answers Ezra Pound's call to "make it new." This radical break with Realism and the Enlightenment ideal of an omniscient, reliable narrator occurs between WWI and WWII in works by authors like Eliot, Pound, Joyce, Woolf, Faulkner, Cummings, and Stein. Influenced by Freudian psychology, authors turn subjective, examining inner states rather than the external world. Reflecting the breakdown of prewar tradition, the style is fragmented in both narrative approach and portrayal of characters. The stream-of-consciousness style imitates a character's rambling thoughts and free associations. Everything is relative; alienated antiheroes confront, with high-brow gravitas, cultural collapse. Technique is experimental, relying on poetic imagery as a vehicle of expression and myth as underlying structure. The Modernists' rejection of traditional practice causes howls of outrage from the public, censorship, suppression, even riots.

1932 James T. Farrell publishes *Young Lonigan*, 1st in brutally realistic trilogy based on Chicago youth Studs Lonigan. Although Farrell depicts influence of South Side environment on character, he insists, "Freedom is my concern," as well as "the dream that each and all have the opportunity to rise to the full stature of their potential humanity." In novels, individuals struggle to overcome social forces and to find true identity and home. Studs is defeated by limited ambition: "to be strong and tough," leader of local gang. He dies young, without political insight or emotional growth. Spiritual, not economic, poverty is American author's subject.

1933 American writer Gertrude Stein publishes her autobiography titled *The Autobiography of Alice B. Toklas* (her companion of 40 years.) Stein leads expatriate group in Paris, "the place that suited those of us that were to create the 20th century art and literature." She discovers *métier* when she begins to write: "Slowly I was knowing that I was a genius." Radically original technique aims to "utter" a subject in language and rhythm of a character's world. Circling reiterations, meandering phrases, simple, monosyllabic words, and idiosyncratic

syntax and punctuation create effect of an instant's experience of complex emotional state. More interested in form than content, style is verbal equivalent of cubism. Shown, Gertrude Stein at right with Alice B. Toklas.

> Every masterpiece has come into the world with a dose of ugliness in it. This ugliness is a sign of the creator's struggle to say something new.
> —Gertrude Stein

1933 Stephen Spender publishes *Poems*, full of bewilderment, uncertainty. He notes that "with poetry one is less sure than with anything else." Poems are like "faceted crystals" as they try to grasp something true within a shifting world: "Never being but always at the edge of being." Uses traditional poetics but modern vocabulary in quest to know, to joust against what he calls The Destructive Element, "an all-pervading Present, which is a world without belief." Replacement offered is a refuge "naked . . . of all except the heart." Famous poem starts, "I think continually of those who were truly great." Ends with "Born of the sun, they traveled a short while towards the sun, / And left the vivid air signed with their honor."

1933 Federico García Lorca's verse play *Blood Wedding* is performed in Madrid. In contrast to naturalistic theater of 19th century, Lorca infuses poetry and symbols into drama. Butterflies, horses represent inevitable

failure and death, due to intervention of hidden forces. Translates traditional ballads, folktales into modern idiom; work shuttles between tragedy and farce, inspiring laughter and tears. *Blood Wedding* includes fantastic players, like personification of Moon and Death, but real human passions. Although inescapable destiny overwhelms all, character says, "Better dead with the blood drained away than alive with it rotting." At age 37 Lorca is murdered by Fascists, his body thrown in unmarked grave.

1933 Octavio Paz publishes 1st book of poems, *Forest Moon*, at 19. Mexican poet's work is erotic, lyrical; expresses attempts to overcome loneliness of human condition through communion, love, and faith. Imagery draws on Mexican past and landscape. In nonfiction essays and books, analyzes Latin American politics, literature, and history. His 1990 Nobel Prize citation praises "impassioned writing with wide horizons, characterized by sensuous intelligence and humanistic integrity."

1934 Robert Graves writes historical novel *I, Claudius*. As a poet, he writes lucid, conversational, tidy poetry and scolds peers like Pound, Yeats, and Eliot for obscure, difficult-to-decipher poems. Early war poems, like "Recalling War," are best, refusing to glorify warfare. On his 1st night patrol, Graves

crawls on his belly for 2 hours, deep into German territory, beneath barbed wire and enemy flares, to retrieve a flask that contains only wine dregs and rainwater. Although the prize proves irrelevant to the outcome of the war, Graves is praised for valor on a dangerous mission. Teaches at Cairo University, accompanied by wife, Laura Riding, a poet; later lives as expatriate on Majorca.

1934 Armenian-American William Saroyan's Impressionistic short stories in *The Daring Young Man on the Flying Trapeze* win acclaim. Theme of stories, novels, plays is immigrant's search for home. Most popular socially conscious play is *The Time of Your Life* (1939); exalts ideals of brotherly love and compassion for the unfortunate.

1935 Bulgarian-born Elias Canetti publishes only novel, *The Tower of Babel*. Portrays insane recluse, lured from his library, who faces grotesque horrors of world. In despair, he returns to refuge and burns himself and books. Canetti lives and works all over Europe, describes life in autobiographical books written in German. Fascinated with relation of individual to masses and nature of communication. Studies psychopathology of crowds, monomania, man's contemptible will to power, fear of death, and reluctance to embrace freedom. Receives Nobel Prize in 1981.

1935 Clifford Odets becomes superstar at age 28 with 1st full-length play, *Awake and Sing*. Uses wisecracking language of street in ricocheting machine-gun tempo: "Diphtheria gets more respect than me!" Biting dialogue echoes brutality of life under failed capitalism of Depression. Tough talk matches heartbreak of American Dream gone bust: "Here without a dollar you don't look the world in the eye," matriarch of play says. "Talk from now to next year—this is life in America." U.S. House Committee on Un-American Activities lists Odets as affiliated with Communist Party in 1947. He cooperates, "naming names," and writes for Hollywood rather than stage, no longer the rebel-hero.

1937 Danish author Isak Dinesen's *Out of Africa* is pastoral account, in English, of her life in Kenya on coffee plantation. A rebel against bourgeois life, in Africa she finds long-sought bliss: "Here at long last one was in a position not to give a damn for all conventions, here was a new kind of freedom which until then one had only found in dreams!" When forced to sell farm, she returns to Denmark, where she creates luminous, lucid prose that rivals the purity she sees in natural landscape of African rift valley.

I had a farm in Africa at the foot of the Ngong Hills. . . . The chief feature of the landscape, and of your life in it, was the air. Looking back on a sojourn in the African highlands, you are struck by your feeling of having lived for a time up in the air. . . . In the middle of the day the air was alive over the land, like a flame burning; it scintillated, waved and shone like running water, mirrored and doubled all objects. . . . Up in this high air you breathed easily, drawing in a vital assurance and lightness of heart. In the highlands you woke up in the morning and thought: Here I am, where I ought to be.   —Isak Dinesen, *Out of Africa*

1937 Zora Neale Hurston publishes novel *Their Eyes Were Watching God*. Tells story of Janie Starks's quest "to the horizon and back," looking for identity, independence, and fulfillment. First Negro to be admitted to Barnard College, Hurston studies anthropology at Columbia. Langston Hughes says of her, "Only to reach a wider audience, need she ever write books —she is a perfect book of entertainment in herself." Autobiography, *Dust Tracks on a Road*, and anthropological works on Deep South document dialect, folklore, and voodoo in vivid accounts of black life. Hurston calls folklore "the boiled-down juice of human living." She dies penniless, buried in unmarked grave.

1938 Paul Éluard's *Cours Naturel* vividly depicts barbarism of bombardment of Guernica during Spanish Civil War in which approximately 1,650 civilians are massacred. Leading figure in both Dada and Surrealism, French poet adapts dream and nightmare imagery in poetry.

1939 Poems of Welsh bard Dylan Thomas in *The Map of Love* seem like wild shouts but are carefully crafted. Spender calls him "a linguistic genius." Style is tempestuous; expresses frenzy of struggle. In stirring recitals, Thomas chants poems with intense passion. (Not a man for moderation, he says poems should be read either very softly or very loudly.) Narrative poems intended as "movement from an overclothed blindness to a naked vision." Dialectical imagery views life as journey to death. Famous poem about father's death, "Do not go gentle into that good night, / Rage, rage against the dying of the light," foreshadows poet's latter years of alcoholism, with beer and brandy for breakfast. Collapses after celebrating 39th birthday at White Horse Tavern (shown). "His life was short and shining as he wanted it," Robert Lowell writes. "Thomas wanted to live burning, burning out."

1939 Nathanael West publishes satiric novel *Day of the Locust*. New Yorker West departs from prevailing

realism in fiction; adds fantasy and allegory. Admits his novels, full of dread and anticipated violence, contain "nothing to root for." Books portray caricatures of tortured dreamers. *The Day of the Locust* draws on American author's experience as Hollywood scriptwriter. Apocalyptic riot erupts outside movie premiere. Hero's painting foreshadows vision of Armageddon, corrupted by hatred, lust for sex and money, insanity of religious cults. West believes Americans are so bored, they seek sensational spectacle to enliven empty lives. "Nothing can ever be violent enough to make taut their slack minds and bodies."

1939 John Steinbeck's sympathy for migrant workers and "Okie" farmers displaced by Dust Bowl shines through in masterpiece novel *The Grapes of Wrath*. Aim is to "set down his time as nearly as he can understand it." Writer should be "the watchdog of society" with duty "to satirize its silliness, to attack its injustices, to stigmatize its faults." Tales of the downtrodden masses affirm nobility of solidarity, which will enable the dispossessed to endure and prevail. Lyrical prose embodies colloquial speech of California workers.

1939 Bertolt Brecht writes expressionist play *Mother Courage and Her Children*. Heroine pulls wagon with goods to sell to soldiers during Thirty Years' War. She refuses to take sides, only wishing to sell her wares: "They called me Courage because I was scared of financial ruin, . . . so I drove my wagon straight through the cannon fire at Riga, with fifty loaves of bread turning moldy, I didn't see that I had a choice." In morally decadent, capitalist world, survival is only possible aim. Refusing love, she hitches herself to wagon, alone, a life force without hope. German Marxist playwright develops radical staging techniques to agitate for political change; intentionally confounds expectations of realism. Shown, poster for *The Threepenny Opera*.

1939 English poet W. H. Auden emigrates to U.S., writes "Sept. 1, 1939." Auden is part of group in late 1920s and early '30s that pioneers new attitudes and techniques in poetry, as England slips into economic depression and stagnation. His early work diagnoses ills of country with cunning irreverence

and verbal clowning. (Marianne Moore calls it "circumspectly audacious.") Only cure for social decay is "In the deserts of the heart / Let the healing fountain start. . . ." Combines popular speech and references to pop culture with formal technique, fusing down-to-earth language with sophisticated versification. Characteristic style: shifts between serious and playful, classical and colloquial.

Writers on the Left

From the late 1940s to late '50s, the U.S. House of Representatives' HUAC (House Un-American Activities Committee) holds hearings to identify and purge "fellow travelers" considered sympathetic to the Communist cause. During the Cold War, a Red Scare causes right-wing conservatives to fear lefty writers. HUAC and Sen. Joseph McCarthy conduct separate witch hunts, spurring Arthur Miller to write his allegory of group hysteria, *The Crucible.* Many notable Hollywood screenwriters and authors are blacklisted and lose their livelihoods during the '50s.

1939 Lillian Hellman's play *The Little Foxes* opens on Broadway. Best-known play treats conflicts within Southern family. Encouraged to write by her partner Dashiell Hammett, Hellman adapts scandal of teachers accused of lesbian affair in 1st play, *The Children's Hour* (1934). Frankness of taboo subject makes play notorious success. Left-wing author subpoenaed to appear before House Un-American Activities Committee in 1952. Refuses

to finger associates in theater who'd been sympathetic to Communism in 1930s, saying, "I cannot and will not cut my conscience to fit this year's fashions." Blacklisted, she's forced to sell her home as Hammett is sentenced to prison.

1939 Jean Giraudoux's play *Ondine* performed. French playwright's young, innocent females represent ideals of truth, nature, and divinity. *Ondine* is tragic story of water spirit (shown in fountain) and her doomed love for a human

knight. Growing up or falling in love entails entrance into "terrible convent of human beings" with inevitable pain and suffering. As Ondine takes on human form in order to marry knight, she loses supernatural power. Mixing fantasy with classical tragedy, Giraudoux examines relations between men and women, incompatible worlds of reality and spirit. Shows gulf between man and pure nature. Compassionate view of adult world conveyed in elegant, extravagant style that impels audience to laugh and cry.

1939 Southern American writer Katherine Anne Porter gains reputation as impeccable stylist in short stories published in *Pale Horse, Pale Rider.* Stories deal with guilt and spiritual sterility of society poised on brink of change. "I am a grandchild of a lost war, and I have blood-knowledge of what life can be in a defeated country on the bare bones of privation." Describes growing up in South at turn of century when sense of family, history, propriety still strong, but confrontations with forces of modernity occur. Writing is simple, disciplined, precise, and economical.

1939 Eugenio Montale's *Occasions* collection of poems appears. Italian poet pushes poetry into modern age with style combining archaic words, scientific

terminology, and idiomatic speech. Deals with moral dilemmas in philosophic poems, focusing on "pain of living" and trying to make poetry effective means to comment on and cope with human problems. This lifelong opponent of fascism says, "The idea of writing for the so-called happy few was never mine. In reality art is always for everyone and for no one." In 1975, he receives Nobel Prize for Literature "for his distinctive poetry which, with great artistic sensitivity, has interpreted human values under the sign of an outlook on life with no illusions."

1940 Soviet author Mikhail Bulgakov writes novel *The Master and Margarita*, which is suppressed and not published until 1966. Author of novels and plays, including satirical comedies, protests when his works are forbidden in Russia after 1927. *Master* is fantasy satire describing 1930s

mass frenzy and paranoia when Devil visits Stalin's Moscow. Famous line: "Manuscripts don't burn." (Bulgakov himself burns early draft of novel to avoid persecution, rewrites it from memory.)

1940 Richard Wright's novel *Native Son* is popular and critical success. "The day *Native Son* appeared, American culture was changed forever," writes critic Irving Howe. "It made impossible a repetition of the old lies." Wright becomes 1st African American on best-seller list, as novel sells a quarter-million copies in 1st month. Traces powerful story of black youth in Chicago slums condemned to tragic fate because of race. Wright's masterpiece is moving autobiography *Black Boy* (1945), which recounts his youth from birth in sharecropper cabin in Mississippi. Embittered by lack of racial progress, Wright emigrates to France.

1940 Carson McCullers's *The Heart Is a Lonely Hunter*, written at 22, is published. American author populates tales with Southern Gothic staples, like humpback dwarf and half-witted deaf mute. Tennessee Williams explains his friend's use of warped characters: "symbols of the grotesque and violent" to express "an underlying dreadfulness in modern experience." Physically deformed and psychologically perverted characters illustrate human incompleteness and hopelessness. Constant theme is loneliness in world of unrequited love. Characters in her most popular novel, *The Member of the Wedding* (1946), less freakish but still yearn for love and acceptance.

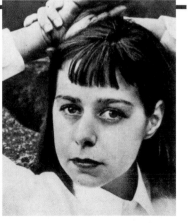

1941 James Agee, commissioned by *Fortune* magazine, turns article into powerfully moving book *Let Us Now Praise Famous Men*. During Depression, writers produce documentary nonfiction expressing American consciousness during tragic period. Writers and photographers join forces to explore back roads and towns in firsthand studies of hard times. New genre of "picture book" emerges. Agee's poetic text capturing inner lives of impoverished Alabama sharecroppers is accompanied by Walker Evans's photos of Hale County farmers.

Existentialism in the 1940s

"Existence precedes essence" is the creed of philosophical writers termed Existentialists. Beginning with nothing, man shapes himself, freely choosing his actions and, therefore, responsible for their consequences. Abandoning all illusions of preordained meaning in life, each individual creates his own code of values. Sartre's "man of good faith" accepts nothingness but does not withdraw. He's engaged, acting for the common good. Camus's "man of the absurd" admits the loneliness of the human condition, faced with the silence of universe, but rejects despair, committed to living in a diminished world.

1943 Jean-Paul Sartre publishes philosophical work *Being and Nothingness*. Causes sensation with dualistic outlook and last phrase that man "is a useless passion." His play *No Exit* (1944) demonstrates existential dilemma; takes place in hell, defined as "other people," with whom characters are trapped.

1941 Eudora Welty's *A Curtain of Green* solidly grounded in Mississippi mud; reflects heritage and local lore. "The art that speaks most clearly, explicitly, directly, and passionately from its place of origin," she says, "will remain the longest understood." Describes outer life of South in language rich with metaphors and symbols and inner life of human beings through often comic confrontations. Imagistic, ironic writing conveys atmosphere, as in picture of car rattling down dirt lane, coughing up "pale sobered winter dust where it chunked out behind like big squashes down the road." Welty's ear for folk idiom of planters, sharecroppers, moonshiners, and white trash is perfect. Door-to-door saleswoman admonishes customer: "It is not Christian or sanitary to put feathers in a vase."

1942 Albert Camus publishes 1st novel, *The Stranger*. Born in Algeria, Camus sets story in French Northern Africa. Protagonist Meursault kills Arab as reflexive reaction to glaring sun reflecting off knife. Meursault is convicted more for lack of emotion at mother's funeral; sentenced to die because of absence of emotional affect and refusal to conform to social expectations. In "The Myth of Sisyphus," Sisyphus is condemned to futile task of pushing stone, which always tumbles down, up mountain. He's archetype of "absurd hero" who finds solace in activity itself and sensuous nature. *The Fall* (1956) examines man's guilt and freedom in godless universe.

1944 Argentinean Jorge Luis Borges publishes short story collections *Fictions* and, in 1949, *The Aleph. Labyrinth* collection makes him superstar when translated into English, even though playful short stories are full of obscure mental puzzles. A professor of English in Buenos Aires, Borges writes in imaginative style known as *Lo*

Fantástico, a precursor of Magic Realism that blurs the boundaries between the ordinary and fantasy. (Two other giants of Argentinean fiction are Julio Cortázar, whose experimental novel *Hopscotch* is his most famous, and Ernesto Sábato, author of dark existentialist novella *The Tunnel* (1948).

1944 Jean Anouilh's *Antigone* opens in Nazi-occupied Paris. French dramatist's major theme is "great thirst for purity." Juxtaposes opposites like fantasy vs. practicality, wealth vs. poverty. *Antigone*, produced despite censorship, is allegory of France under Nazi collaborators of Vichy regime. Antigone denounces King Creon: "You with your promise of a humdrum happiness—provided a person doesn't ask much of life. I want everything of life, I do; and I want it now! . . . I want to be sure of everything this very day; sure that everything will be as beautiful as when I was a little girl. If not, I want to die!"

1945 Gwendolyn Brooks's superbly crafted poems in *A Street in Bronzeville* display sophisticated technique, verbal wit coupled with consciousness of racial inequity. She is 1st African American to win Pulitzer Prize (for 2nd volume of poems, *Annie Allen*, in 1950). Brooks passionately and compassionately describes human aspirations and dilemmas. Poems reflect African-American experience in Chicago ghettos, as in mother's heartbreaking lament for aborted babies: "You were born, you had body, you died. / It is just that you never giggled or planned or cried. / Believe me I loved you all. / Believe me I knew you, though faintly, and I loved you, I loved you / All."

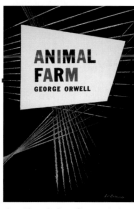

1945 A socialist who's committed to true equality, George Orwell attacks Stalinism and totalitarianism in *Animal Farm*. Brilliant satire on Soviet history is his 1st success; portrays perversion of communist ideal, noting that, in practice, "All Animals Are Equal, But Some Animals Are More Equal Than Others." Dystopian novel *Nineteen Eighty-four* (1949) suggests disturbing idea that Soviet thought control could be established everywhere. Novels all deal with sociopolitical issues more than individual characters. Writes with total honesty, called "the conscience of his generation" by V. S. Pritchett.

1946 Robert Penn Warren publishes *All the King's Men*, study of flawed politician based on corrupt

Louisiana demagogue Huey Long (shown, Broderick Crawford as fictional governor Willie Stark in 1949 movie with John Ireland and Joanne Dru). Popular novel dissects competing claims of practicality and idealism, seen through eyes of narrator Jack Burden, who's both attracted to Stark's charisma and vision and repelled by his expediency. American writer's poetry notable for brilliant use of metaphor and descriptive power. Joins narrative and lyric to convey moral dilemmas of modern world with great intensity.

The Fugitives

A group of "Fugitive" poets in Nashville, Tennessee —part of a Southern literary renaissance—forms after WWI. Leaders are John Crowe Ransom, Donald Davidson, Laura Riding, Robert Penn Warren, and Allen Tate. To forge authentic new forms, they question the culture of their region. In 1930, the Fugitives publish *I'll Take My Stand*, a defense of values associated with the South's agrarian roots, in opposition to rampant industrialization and urbanization. The Fugitives insist art should not proselytize for political ideology or substitute for religion, a foundation of the New Criticism.

1946 Eugene O'Neill's *The Iceman Cometh* portrays haunted character struggling to admit reality. After experimental, Expressionistic plays, O'Neill turns to dramatic realism, producing theatrical experiences of searing intensity. Strikes mother lode when he mines tortured-family dynamics in plays like *A Touch of the Poet* and his masterpiece, *A Long Day's Journey into Night*. O'Neill's pessimistic view of world as site of suffering is leavened by beauty of characters' poetic dialogue, uttered in extremity of pain. Sinclair Lewis (1st American to win Nobel Prize for Literature) says that O'Neill (2nd American to win) changed American theater "utterly in 10 or 12 years from a false world of neat and competent trickery into a world of splendor and fear and greatness."

1947 Tennessee Williams' *A Streetcar Named Desire* opens in brilliant production with Marlon Brando as Stanley Kowalski. (Shown, Vivien Leigh as Blanche DuBois in 1951 film.) *The Glass Menagerie* (1945), Williams's 1st hit, establishes theme of lonely characters defeated by harsh reality, dreamers overwhelmed by decay. *Cat on a Hot Tin Roof* (1955) rails against "mendacity" and destructive delusions. Southern playwright breaks taboos by dealing with subjects like rape, alcoholism, homosexuality, cannibalism, nymphomania. Extreme characters portrayed through compelling—often poetic—language, beautiful imagery, effective action, visual and aural effects that go beyond "the exhausted theater of realism." Although characters seem exaggerated, their psychic pain is tangible. Best outcome amid chaos is dignified acceptance.

1946 William Carlos Williams publishes 1st installment of long personal epic *Paterson*, catalog of scenes, images, and snippets from American history clustered around New Jersey mill town. Poetry appears spontaneous, formless, and "antipoetic" in its simplicity, directness, aversion to abstraction. Portrays squalor and splendor of urban America. Williams, a physician for 40 years, announces doctrine: "No ideas but in things." Innovative verse breaks with stuffy poetic conventions and erudite rhetoric to "ruffle the skirts of prudes" with immediate, concrete renderings of sensory experience. Most famous poem: "The Red Wheel Barrow."

1946 Nikos Kazantzakis dramatizes competing claims of Apollo and Dionysus in novel *Zorba the Greek*. Torn between flesh and spirit, Kazantzakis's characters show dual nature of humanity. Hero, Zorba, represents vital life force, contrasted to timid narrator who contemplates life from a distance rather than living fully. (Shown, Anthony Quinn in title role with Alan Bates in 1964 film.) Author's epitaph reads: "I hope for nothing. I fear nothing. I am free."

1948 Truman Capote's 1st novel, *Other Voices, Other Rooms*, published when Southern author is 24, shows gift for lush language and literary style.

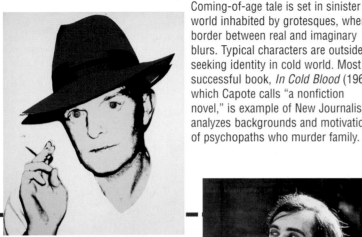

Coming-of-age tale is set in sinister world inhabited by grotesques, where border between real and imaginary blurs. Typical characters are outsiders seeking identity in cold world. Most successful book, *In Cold Blood* (1966), which Capote calls "a nonfiction novel," is example of New Journalism; analyzes backgrounds and motivations of psychopaths who murder family.

1949 French thinker Simone de Beauvoir's *The Second Sex* is central to development of modern feminism. Analyzes women's 2nd-class status,

defined as "the other," deviant from male ideal that dominates society. *The Coming of Age* (1972) is penetrating portrayal of old age. Earlier Existentialist writings deal with conundrum of freedom in godless world and necessity to act and define oneself: "The human species is forever in a state of change, forever becoming." A longtime companion of Jean-Paul Sartre, de Beauvoir is leading leftist intellectual in postwar France.

1948 Antonin Artaud dies, French writer and actor who argues for "theater of cruelty" in 1932 manifesto. Artaud, seen in 1926 film *The Wandering Jew*, demands ceremonial ritual in drama. Influence more important than output, since Beckett, Ionesco, Genet, and

Albee develop his ideas. Artaud rejects psychological and narrative realism; prefers "Total Theater," in which gesture, action, lighting, set design, and movement—rather than dialogue—express message. Aim: to make theater disturbing and liberating. Believes myths and archetypes portray inner human conflict. Drama should be improvisational assault on senses, eliminating "third wall" between spectator and actor to "inundate" audience with awareness of man's evil tendencies.

Feminist Literature

In the 1960s and '70s, the influence of Simone de Beauvoir's *Second Sex* spurs a spate of writers to re-examine women's roles through a new perspective, the "raised consciousness" of the women's liberation movement. Critical and scholarly writing analyzes the role of gender stereotypes, as in Betty Friedan's *The Feminine Mystique* (1963), Germaine Greer's *The Female Eunuch* (1970), and in the pages of Gloria Steinem's *Ms.* magazine (founded in 1971). Creative authors linked to feminism are Doris Lessing, Adrienne Rich, Tillie Olsen, and Erica Jong.

1949 Arthur Miller's *Death of a Salesman* kicks up controversy about whether common man can be tragic hero. Traveling salesman Willy Loman loses faith in American dream. False values corrode his confidence, inspiring wife's impassioned plea: "I don't say he's a great man. . . . But he's a human being, and a terrible thing is happening to him. So attention must be paid." Play describes salesman as archetypal dreamer: "a man way out there in the blue, riding on a smile and a shoeshine. And when they start not smiling back—that's an earthquake." Miller's plays concerned with self-realization and search for truth.

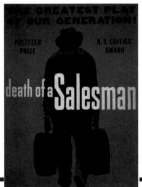

1949 Jean Genet's *The Maids* has Paris premiere, 2 years after he's released from life sentence in prison through intervention of Sartre and Cocteau. A prostitute and much-convicted thief, Genet writes novels and plays based on lurid underworld experiences. Plays like *The Balcony* and *The Blacks* present bitter frustrations and hypocrisy of society where good and evil are ambiguous. In stylized, ritualistic action, outcast characters fight against stereotypes and oppression but fail to gain release. French playwright, allied with Theater of the Absurd and Theater of Cruelty, celebrates beauty of evil, portrays homosexuality and criminality in deliberately provocative style to subvert conventional morality.

1950 Romanian-born French playwright Eugene Ionesco's 1st play, *The Bald Soprano*, defines Theater of the Absurd. Ionesco cultivates irrationality in absurdist dramas with flagrant non sequiturs, bizarre transformations, and violations of logic. Plays are farcical more than bitter, revealing longing for love and communion. *The Rhinoceros* (1959) is allegory of rise of Nazis to power, where hero feels pressure to conform to bestiality of his peers who turn into rhinos. In *Amédée* (1954), couple lives with corpse, emblem of dead love, which swells to grotesque size during play.

1950

1950 William Inge's 2nd play, *Come Back, Little Sheba*, is hit, especially in film version with Shirley Booth and Burt Lancaster. Title refers to wife calling for lost puppy but her cry is plea for relief from dreary life; character must relinquish hope of return to happier days. Midwestern American writer's plays

dramatize trapped lives of frustration, emptiness, sorrow, sexual tension in heartland of America. "I regard a play as a composition rather than a story, as a distillation of life rather than a narration of it."

Theater of the Absurd

Avant-garde theatrical productions that reveal the illogic and meaninglessness of life spring from the Theater of the Absurd movement. Outrageous, irrational, grotesque, often violent, these plays use nonverbal means like costume, gesture, masks, sounds, and stylized movement more than straightforward dialogue and narrative. Antonin Artaud, Jarry, Beckett, Genet, Ionesco, Pinter, and Albee place characters in hostile environments, which they're helpless to understand or control. Their themes are big issues like alienation, loneliness, decay, and lack of purpose, coherence, and freedom. Their outlandish approach shocks and distances the audience rather than spurring identification with characters' dilemmas.

1951 J. D. Salinger's novel *The Catcher in the Rye* deals with precocious, disturbed adolescents, whose sensitivity and innocence contrast with sterile adult world. Humor, 1st-person colloquial speech, and deadpan irony delight readers, but Salinger retires from publishing in mid-1960s. *Catcher*'s hero, Holden Caulfield, denounces "phoniness": "Take most people, they're crazy about cars. They worry if they get a little scratch on them, and they're always talking about how many miles they get to a gallon, and if they get a brand-new car already they start thinking about trading it in for one that's even newer. I don't even like old cars, I mean they don't even interest me. I'd rather have a goddam horse. A horse is at least human, for God's sake."

1951 Italian Alberto Moravia publishes novel *The Conformist*. Existentialist novelist sees work banned and seized during fascist years before WWII. To avoid censorship, he writes allegorical, surrealist tales. After liberation in 1944, he returns to Rome and his Neo-Realist works become popular. Deals with aridity and decadence of middle-class life, alienation, and political issues. Style is stark, employing simple vocabulary and inner monologue.

1951 Marianne Moore's *Collected Poems* wins Pulitzer Prize. Devoted baseball fan is called by Elizabeth Bishop "The World's Greatest Living Observer" for omnivorous variety of her poetic subjects. Sharp eye for detail and meticulous craft create poems ranging from Imagistic to Metaphysical. American writer embeds poems with quotations called "collections of flies in amber." Her verse fulfils Eliot's view of goal of Imagist poetry: "to induce a peculiar concentration upon something visual, and to set in motion an expanding succession of concentric feelings." Intensifies feeling by simplifying expression.

1952 Flannery O'Connor's novel *Wise Blood* presents deranged Hazel Motes, who preaches "church of Christ without Christ, where the blind don't see, the lame don't walk and what's dead stays that way." Novels and short stories are set among red clay and rednecks of rural Georgia, a landscape soaked in violence, mordant humor, sin, and salvation. Grotesque characters are haunted by religion, portrayed in vivid images and colloquial dialect. Bizarre goings-on seem commonplace, as when Hulga Hopewell is duped into losing her wooden leg to a shyster Bible salesman. Masterful short story collections are *A Good Man Is Hard to Find* and *Everything That Rises Must Converge*. A faithful Roman Catholic, O'Connor infuses fiction with what she calls "sacramental view of life."

1952 Ralph Ellison's novel *The Invisible Man* employs rich diversity of African-American speech and folktales. Hero initially believes in Horatio Alger myth of advancement through merit; gradually learns of inevitable chaos, prejudice, and repression in American race relations. Black hero is "invisible man" because others see not his reality but their preconceived notions.

1952 Irish writer Samuel Beckett writes *Waiting for Godot* in French; translates it into English in 1955. Vaudeville-influenced *Waiting for Godot* is plotless play in which two tramps, Vladimir and Estragon, wait in bleak landscape for promised appearance of Godot, who never comes. All fractured talk and no action, anticipation without fulfillment, the play represents despair of modern life, coupled with need to persevere in face of emptiness. Comic grotesquery disguises fear of sterility.

1953 James Baldwin's autobiographical novel, *Go Tell It on the Mountain,* published. African-American author's frequent themes are racial injustice and coming to terms with homosexuality. During civil rights struggles, writes forceful essays like *The Fire Next Time (1963)* and novel *Another Country (1962),* evincing anxiety about deteriorating race relations. Work becomes bitter and angry; warns of racial strife but pleads to avoid violence and animosity. A 1963 letter to nephew says: "You can only be destroyed by believing that you really are what the white world calls a nigger." Concludes: "We cannot be free until [our brothers] are free." African Americans must "cease fleeing from reality and begin to change it."

I wake to sleep, and take my waking slow. I feel my fate in what I cannot fear. I learn by going where I have to go.
—Theodore Roethke,
The Waking

1953 Theodore Roethke's poetry collection *The Waking* awarded Pulitzer Prize. American poet's father was a florist; weird beauty of greenhouse proves source of imagery in poems like "Cuttings" and "Root Cellar." Early work more orthodox in format, rational and ironic in mood. Later develops expansive, loose forms influenced by Whitman and gives free reign to mystical love of nature and Emersonian Transcendentalism. W. H. Auden says, "Many people have the experience of feeling physically soiled and humiliated by life; . . . but both to remember and to transform its humiliation into something beautiful, as Mr. Roethke does, is rare."

1953 Canadian-born Saul Bellow publishes picaresque novel *The Adventures of Augie March.* Features familiar antihero: spiritually famished, exuberant, in search of beauty, love, meaning, and identity. *Herzog* and *Henderson the Rain King* also crammed with comic-philosophical speculations on absurdity of human condition. Bellow, longtime Chicago resident, views human folly with broad intelligence and depth of feeling. Characters both pure and puny. Prose captures bustle of pulsating world. Calling *Augie March* the Great American Novel "because of its fantastic inclusiveness, its pluralism, its qualmless promiscuity," British novelist Martin Amis notes, "Everything is here, the crushed and the exalted and all the notches in between."

1954 Life insurance company executive Wallace Stevens publishes *Collected Poems.* Work is revolutionary, using experimental styles, exotic symbols, rich imagery, ambiguous titles, odd analogies. "To make a new intelligence prevail," American poet turns to novel material. Because of difficulty and inscrutability of his poems, he's called "a virtuoso of the inane" who writes "near

nonsense." Aims not just at daring originality but revelation of decay of traditional values and confusions of modern era. Work is preoccupied with relation between real and ideal, inner and outer spheres. Offers new mythology, "supreme fiction" of imagination to fill void of lost faith. Words have almost incantatory sensuality.

Jewish-American Novel

Besides Bellow, Bernard Malamud, Philip Roth, and Isaac Bashevis Singer produce outstanding novels and short stories drawing on their Jewish heritage in the 1950s to '80s. Polish-born Singer emigrates to New York in 1935 and writes grotesque but realistic tales, in Yiddish, fusing Jewish culture with universal concerns. A student of the kabbalah, he shows the conflict between mysticism and cynicism in short story collections like *Gimpel the Fool* (1957). Malamud captures the Jewish-American idiom, treating the need for solidarity coupled with the experience of loneliness. *The Fixer* (1966) deals with a Jewish handyman, persecuted by anti-Semites, in Tsarist Russia. Roth protests, "The epithet American-Jewish writer has no meaning for me. If I'm not an American, I'm nothing." Yet his works dramatize issues of Jewish identity, caught between the need to shape one's own identity and ties to the past and family. His novella *Goodbye, Columbus* (1959) satirizes, with earthy humor, American ideals and their betrayal. Looking at the plight of post-immigrants in the melting pot of Protestant America, the notorious novel *Portnoy's Complaint* (1969) portrays striving to realize the American dream, to fit in yet retain one's individuality.

1954 Harriette Arnow's novel *The Dollmaker* is 3rd book in her Kentucky trilogy. Best seller and critical success is considered her masterpiece. Traces Appalachian woman transplanted to inhospitable soil of Detroit factory life.

Heartbreaking story focuses on strong matriarch's struggles in alien environment, with convincing regional dialect and vivid characters. Novel *Hunter's Horn* (1949), set in mountains of eastern Kentucky, compares fate of larger-than-life fox called King Devil, obsessively hunted by trophy seekers, to struggle of female character seeking to escape stifling society and the trap of biology.

1955 Vladimir Nabokov's scandalous novel *Lolita* depicts middle-aged narrator torn by love and lust for 12-year-old nymphet: "Lolita, light of my life, fire of my loins. My sin, my soul." Although book, considered obscene, not published in U.S. until 1958, theme is satirical quest for innocence and the superiority of aesthetics to crass world. Russian-born American novelist is ardent butterfly collector and brilliant prose stylist. Works marked by parody, wit, elegant style, paradox, inventive word play, erudition. Shown, opening lines

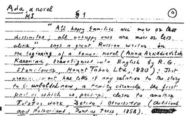

of *Ada, or Ardor: A Family Chronicle*, novel that also deals with sexual obsession.

Beat Literature

The Beat movement emerges on both coasts of 1950s America. The term, invented by novelist Jack Kerouac, reflects different connotations of the word "beat": beatific, down-and-out, and throbbing with the beat of modern jazz. Allen Ginsberg chants apocalyptic farewells to the American Dream, Gregory Corso looks at the world as an outsider in his colloquial poems, Gary Snyder presents his reverence for nature in Zen haikus, and Lawrence Ferlinghetti's poetry is both wry and surreal. Others considered Beats are novelist William S. Burroughs, and poets Robert Creeley, Michael McClure, and Kenneth Rexroth. Their subject is the need to move from the philistine falsity of Eisenhower-era complacency toward visionary enlightenment. They aim for transcendence to a higher consciousness, fueled by drugs, alcohol, mysticism, and Zen Buddhism. Their pro-nature, antitechnological stance is very influential on antiwar, counterculture politics of the '60s. They reject middle-class values and stodginess in favor of intense experience.

1956 Allen Ginsberg reads *Howl* in San Francisco gallery, beginning: "I saw the best minds of my generation destroyed by madness, starving hysterical naked, / dragging themselves through the negro streets at dawn looking for an angry fix / angelheaded hipsters burning for the ancient heavenly connection to the starry dynamo in the machinery of night." American poet savagely

denounces materialism, conformity of postwar America; eventually cleared of charge of obscenity in famous trial. Describes alienated youth, termed Beat Generation, in effusive poems influenced by windy lines of Whitman, ecstatic hallucinations of William Blake, mystical pantheism of Transcendentalism.

1956 John Osborne's play *Look Back in Anger* (shown, Richard Burton and Mary Ure in film version) captures disillusionment of postwar English society. Irreverent invective of central character shatters genteel conventions of Edwardian theater. In 4 best plays, British playwright's anger and ridicule spill out of protagonists, causing Osborne to be dubbed "angry young man." "When he had a pen in his hand," says director Peter Hall, "it was like giving a kid a machine gun."

1956 Swiss playwright Friedrich Dürrenmatt's *The Visit* premieres in Zurich. Play is "a tragic comedy," story of wealthy Claire's merciless quest for revenge against former lover and how offer of money for his life corrupts townfolk. Eventually, family, church, law, government, and academia all turn against ex-lover, and he takes responsibility for his crime. World around him is rotten, but he grows into

serenity and self-knowledge. Only death brings freedom. Dürrenmatt says in modern world, "we no longer find tragic heroes, but only tragedies staged by world butchers and carried out by meat-grinding machines."

1957 Lawrence Durrell publishes novel *Justine*, 1st of panoramic *Alexandria Quartet* tetralogy. Born in Indian Himalayas to Irish parents and educated in England, Durrell is world traveler who lives in Corfu with his mother. Before novels make him sensationally successful, he's journalist, instructor, and cabaret pianist. He's on the point of taking a job as sheepherder in South of France before he unexpectedly becomes rich and famous. Called a poet who strayed into prose, writing is moody, mocking, bawdy, and sensuous. He terms *Alexandria Quartet* "a big city poem." It's a study of many forms of modern love, told from different points of view, and of exotic international society.

1957 Boris Pasternak's *Doctor Zhivago*, written in 1955, is published in Italian translation. Negative view of Marxism and Russian Revolution causes sensation when novel is published in English a year later. Furor in Soviet Union forces Pasternak to reject 1958 Nobel Prize. His telegram to Swedish Academy: "In view of the sense that this distinction suffers from in the society which I share, I must renounce the undeserved prize conferred upon me." Pasternak's funeral in 1960 turns into mass demonstration against autocratic regime.

1958 Giuseppe Tomasi's *The Leopard* published 2 years after his death. Sicilian aristocrat, Prince of Lampedusa, writes sole novel at age

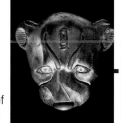

60; describes national events like unification of Italy and Giuseppe Garibaldi's invasion of Sicily through viewpoint of old noble family. Negative portrayal causes vehement debate. Book now recognized as perceptive study of epoch in poetic style. Most famous line delivered by young nephew of aging aristocrat: "Unless we ourselves take a hand now, they'll foist a republic on us. If we want things to stay as they are, things will have to change."

Russian Dissident Literature

Nikita Krushchev, the Soviet leader in the 1950s, fears writers will form "a second government" if their works are freely available. Even under the czars, writers like Pushkin, Dostoyevsky, and Tolstoy were persecuted. In the Soviet era under Joseph Stalin (who died in 1953), writers like Gorky, Pasternak, and Alexander Solzhenitsyn are curtailed and defamed. Denied freedom to move about, write, and publish, they circulate their works clandestinely. Pasternak is forbidden to travel to Sweden to accept the Nobel Prize. Solzhenitsyn's *A Day in the Life of Ivan Denisovich* (1962), which exposes Soviet prisons, is the 1st public acknowledgment of gulag "corrective labor" camps and the secret police penetrating all Soviet life. Reacting against this temporary lapse in censorship, Soviet officials systematically liquidate the intelligentsia, as in the infamous 1964 trial of the poet Joseph Brodsky, convicted as a "social parasite" and condemned to five years' hard labor. In his 1968 *Cancer Ward*, Solzhenitsyn sees a new episode of Stalinization after the brief thaw during the Brezhnev era. He describes one of his characters as "that righteous one without whom, according to the proverb, no village can stand. Nor any city. Nor our whole land." Being a truthful writer in a totalitarian regime requires not just skill, but courage.

1958 Nigerian Chinua Achebe's 1st novel, *Things Fall Apart*, is classic work on African colonialism. With compassion and wisdom, he shows struggles of traditional society to evolve yet retain its heritage. Views writer as conscience of people, with duty to teach and heal. Flashes of wit and satire illuminate complex problems of Africa.

In clear narrative, Achebe uses tribal beliefs, proverbs, fables, and local imagery. "A writer who feels a strong and abiding concern for his fellows cannot evade the role as social critic which is the contemporary expression of commitment to the community."

1959 Günter Grass publishes 1st and best-known novel, *The Tin Drum* (shown, David Bennett as narrator Oskar in 1979 film). Novel is coming-of-age story in which Oskar, a hunchback, recalls events during Hitler era. Suspicious of adult world, at age 3 boy determines to grow no more, beats on drum to express contempt for weak adults—the true freaks—who encourage growth of Nazism. A committed socialist, called the "conscience of Germany," Grass exposes collective guilt. Constant theme of satirical novels combining fact and fantasy is necessity to face truth about German past.

1960

1960 Randall Jarrell publishes poetry collection *The Woman at the Washington Zoo*. Acute critic and gifted professor's theme in poems is change, symbolized by travels, dreams, and fear of death. "Wit, pathos, and brilliance of intelligence," is how Robert Lowell describes Jarrell's poetic gifts, calling him "the most heartbreaking English poet of his generation." Work ranges from realistic (describes death of gunner on fighter plane: "When I died they washed me out of the turret with a hose") to elusive. John Crowe Ransom says of his pupil that Jarrell has "an angel's velocity and range with language." Poems vibrate with energy, emotion, intensity.

1960 Harold Pinter achieves 1st popular success with play *The Caretaker*. Known for realistic dialogue termed "Pinteresque," which consists of non sequiturs, pauses, sentence fragments, repetition. Style conveys ambiguity of communication and multilayered meanings. Plays have atmosphere of menace, illogical actions, lack of rational explanations or clear message. They show slices of life at turning points in characters' lives, where they struggle to define themselves in world where conformity is price of survival. General appearance of order undermined by intrusion of alien element and struggle for dominance. Theme: impossibility of knowing truth.

1961 Joseph Heller's satiric antiwar novel *Catch-22* lends a term to the English language. Based on American author's experience as WWII bombardier, his 1st novel traces antihero Yossarian's attempts to survive lunacy of fanatics in bomber squadron and to return home intact. As absurdity of no-way-out requirements escalates, Yossarian pleads insanity. Doctor invokes Catch-22: anyone "would be crazy to fly more missions and sane if he didn't, but if he was sane, he had to fly them. If he flew them he was crazy and didn't have to; but if he didn't, he was sane and had to."

1962 Edward Albee's searing *Who's Afraid of Virginia Woolf?* makes his reputation as major dramatist. (Film version stars Richard Burton and Elizabeth Taylor, shown, as sparring spouses with secret.) His greatest play displays lacerating repartee and shattering revelations of desperate characters who both manipulate and are manipulated. Typical arc of plays progresses from seeming normalcy to increasing emotional turmoil and bewilderment to peak of intensity, then quick wrap-up. American playwright often explores illusions within family, tangled relationships, struggle for domination, lies of American culture.

1963 Adrienne Rich makes breakthrough into free verse in *Snapshots of a Daughter-in-Law*. Earlier work tighter, with precise form; evolves to more conversational rhythms, natural speech, varied length of stanzas, and looser punctuation. Change is substantive as well as formal. American poet writes: "What we see, we see, / and the seeing is changing." Feminist poems see "patriarchal politics and patriarchal civilization" amid changing roles of men and women. Presents female perspective ("contending with a woman's demons") on quest to fulfill potential, find satisfaction. Increasingly she protests status quo, demands social justice, freedom from oppression. Expresses anger over conflict between duties as wife/mother and artist.

Confessional Poetry

W. D. Snodgrass and Robert Lowell initiate a style of autobiographical poetry in the late 1950s. (Lowell's poems describe his sojourn in a mental hospital and the breakup of his marriage.) In lyrical outpourings, the poets portray anguished experiences in an intensely subjective tone. Although the subject is their personal life and its failures, their themes match the mood of postwar anxiety and disillusionment. Psychic pain is not merely a pose. At least 3 of these poets (John Berryman, Anne Sexton, and Sylvia Plath) commit suicide. As Sexton says of poetry: "It should almost hurt." Plath's poetry, Lowell says, "almost makes one feel . . . that almost all other poetry is about nothing. Still, it's searingly extreme; a triumph by a hair, that one almost wishes had never come about."

1962 Sylvia Plath publishes poems with violent, contradictory emotions in *The Colossus*. Excessively sensitive yet able to turn her emotional extremes into shrieks that encompass a world gone awry, Plath expresses despair and a disintegrating mind possessed by fury. Poems scream with pain, deal forthrightly with suicide attempts, as in "Lady Lazarus": "The second time I meant / To last it out and not come back at all. / I rocked shut / As a seashell. / They had to call and call / And pick the worms off me like sticky pearls." Plath kills herself in 1963 at age 30. Her poems, Robert Lowell writes, "are as extreme as one can bear, rather more so, but whatever wrecked her life somehow gave an edge, freedom and even control, to her poetry."

1964 Robert Lowell moves away from self-exposure of earlier confessional style in *Poems for the Union Dead*. Earlier book *Life Studies* (1959) had signaled new poetic direction toward self-revelation, in which he describes mental breakdown with harrowing candor. Passion smolders in verse, as in lines written in mental hospital: "These are the tranquilized *Fifties*, / And I am forty. Ought I to regret my seed time?" With elegance and technical sophistication, New England poet depicts instability, personal disturbances, guilt. Poems express his protest against degradation of American ideals elliptically, but quest for new grounds of faith is clear.

1964 James Earl Jones, shown, stars off-Broadway in Athol Fugard's *The Blood Knot*. South African playwright explores, with bitter humor, trauma of apartheid and its larger implications in individual's search for identity and justice. *Blood Knot* is 1st play performed in South Africa (1961) with racially mixed cast. Fugard welcomes actors' improvisation in *The Island* (1972), play about infamous Robben Island. Two prisoners work in quarry by day and rehearse *Antigone* in cell by night. Fugard uses improv to avoid prosecution. "Written text," actor John Kani explains, is "evidence to be used [by] a

District Attorney who might lay charges against us. So we kept continuing to improvise according to the interactions and response with the audience. That way we used our life experience, structured it around a story, to take the audience on a journey . . ."

1966 Thomas Pynchon publishes surreal comic novel *The Crying of Lot 49*. "Lot 49" refers to auction of stamp collection. The stamps, "little colored windows into deep vistas of space and time," are "crying" a message about the for-sale legacy of America. Reclusive American's complex novels present pessimistic worldview, where technology dominates and human beings are trapped in unbearable, incomprehensible isolation. Factual details of arcane science densely litter his novels, making distinction between truth and falsity unknowable. Instead of socially evolving through scientific progress, Pynchon shows mankind devolving into chaos. Novels are long, shapeless, rambling conglomerations that mimic overload of technoculture.

1967 Gabriel García Márquez creates imaginary Colombian village in *One Hundred Years of Solitude*. Epic novel, full of humor, invention, and fantasy, traces rise and fall of 7 generations of family, parallel to evolution of Western civilization. In supreme example of Magic Realism, miraculous and real con-

verge. Left-wing author defends poor against domestic and foreign oppression. Ends 1982 Nobel speech with hope for "a new and sweeping utopia of life, where no one will be able to decide for others how they die, where love will prove true and happiness be possible, and where the races condemned to 100 years of solitude will have, at last and forever, a second opportunity on earth."

1968 Alexander Solzhenitsyn publishes abroad his novel *Cancer Ward*, written in 1957 but suppressed by Soviet censors. Solzhenitsyn is sentenced, in 1945, to 8 years in camps for political prisoners, as punishment for disrespectful remark (called Stalin "the boss" in private letter). Exiled to remote Kazakhstan, he is later "rehabilitated" and exile

lifted. After *A Day in the Life of Ivan Denisovich* (1962), based on struggle of prisoners to survive and maintain self-respect in bleak camps, is published, his work is increasingly repressed. The 1970 Nobel Prize for "ethical force" of his work intensifies official attacks on him. Arrested in 1974, Solzhenitsyn leaves for West, doesn't return to Russia until 1994.

Magic Realism

Lo real maravilloso, or Magic Realism, is a literary style associated with Latin American authors like Márquez, Carlos Fuentes, and Mario Vargas Llosa, in which flights of fancy interrupt the description of "real" events in fiction. Impossible occurrences like characters suddenly levitating into the air are presented as if such things occur every day. This narrative technique enriches and extends plot and characters, adding an element of outlandish fantasy to capture the extravagant history, culture, and politics of the region. During the 1960s, Latin American fiction experiences a "boom" of innovation and experimentation. The stories are colorful, exuberant, and accessible, while engaging pressing historical and political themes.

1970 Elizabeth Bishop's *Complete Poems* wins National Book Award. American author assumes stance of detached observer, suggesting more than stating through subtle variations on rhythm and offbeat rhymes. Depicts surface appearance with exactitude, advancing from minutely observed reality to dreamlike flights. Contrasts every-day world with images that spark the mind to higher reflection. Composes poetry like painter with Impressionistic streaks and dabs of description that cohere into larger whole: "The palm trees clatter in the stiff breeze like the bills of the pelicans."

1972 Gonzalo Torrente Ballester's masterpiece *La Saga/Fuga de J.B.* is published. Spanish left-leaning novelist creates imaginary city full of suggestions and evocations, in style akin to Magic Realism. Novel *The Island of the Cut Hyacinths* wins National Literature Prize for its mix of fantasy and reality, humor, imagination, and intelligence.

Postmodern Literature

Postmodernism arises after WWII as a reaction against the serious sense of mission of Modernist writers. Still going strong today, it's a pastiche of irony, cynicism, and self-conscious deconstruction of Meaning. Very self-reflexive, it nevertheless incorporates diverse references, everything from high to low culture. The typical stance of Po-Mo authors is an anti-techno-capitalist spirit and scorn for consumer society where everything becomes a commodity and genuine experience is replaced by spectacle, sensationalism, and simulation. Discontinuity and parody characterize Po-Mo fiction. It challenges standards of decency and reason and explores marginal elements of society. It is often cheeky metafiction, where the falsity of the narrative is overt, using paradox and abrupt shifts to undercut the appearance of reality. Among Postmodern writers are Thomas Pynchon, Don De Lillo, John Fowles, Donald Barthelme, John Barth, Julian Barnes, David Foster Wallace, Vladimir Nabokov, William S. Burroughs, and Dave Eggers.

1972 Margaret Atwood portrays a woman's journey of self-discovery and coming to terms with her past and present in brilliant novel *Surfacing*. Canadian author explores themes of female struggle for autonomy in male-dominated world and for life in harmony with natural rhythms. *The Handmaid's Tale* is dystopian, futuristic view of a woman's fight against misogynistic fascism, which reduces women's status to property. With wry humor and vividly poetic imagery, her work is concerned with human rights, national and personal identity, environmental issues, social myths, and the role of women and their relationships with men.

1981 Umberto Eco's medieval mystery novel *The Name of the Rose* is huge hit. Arcane historical figures and philosophical discourse color intricate plot of tale set in 14th-century monastery. Novel deals with religious controversies and illustrates Postmodernist idea of hypertextuality (interconnection of all literature). Eco is professor of semiotics at University of Bologna, a famed literary theorist who insists on interpreting words in context.

1981   Peruvian Mario Vargas Llosa publishes novel *The War of the End of the World*. Activist writer (shown, campaigning for president in 1990) creates surreal portrait of Peruvian society. *Aunt Julia and the Scriptwriter* (1977) is comic novel on grand scale. Uses device of Magic Realism to incorporate fantastic into the literal. Extravagant, inventive novel *The Green House* shifts time and place in stream-of-consciousness narrative to express how lives intermingle. Characters are saints, sinners, victims who seem to live and breathe. Message: Man, like the jungle, has mysterious, unquenchable energy.

1983   William Kennedy's *Ironweed* appears, after 11 major publishers reject it; wins Pulitzer Prize. Novel is part of 7-novel Albany Cycle, set in the author's birthplace; describes working-class, Irish-American life. Author endows gritty streets and dives with mythic quality of James Joyce's Dublin. *Ironweed* follows skid row bum one weekend during the Depression when he returns to Albany, New York (he'd abandoned it years before, after accidentally causing his infant son's death while drunk). Derelict says, "My guilt is all I have left. If I lose it, I have stood for nothing, done nothing, been nothing." Kennedy's mentor Saul Bellow says, "The people he wrote about didn't know they had become pariahs. He wrote about them from the inside."

1982   Chilean Isabel Allende's *The House of the Spirits* (multigenerational tale of upper-class family) published. Peruvian-born Allende, a proponent of Magic Realism, is 1st major female writer among Latin American Boom authors. Historical novel *Inés of My Soul* (translated, 2006) relates adventures of 16th-century Spanish *conquistadora*, Inés Suárez, who founds 1st Spanish colony in Chile. Allende calls true tale "a work of intuition," but parallels to politics of imperialism are clear. Bloodiest battle occurs on day her uncle, Salvador Allende, then president of Chile, is assassinated. Heroine Inés concludes that violence "exists everywhere. . . . Nothing changes; we humans repeat the same sins over and over, eternally."

1983   In Thomas Bernhard's novel *The Loser*, protagonist and author's alter-ego is pianist Glenn Gould, shown. In novels and plays, Austrian writer mocks and mourns country's Nazi past. "All my life," he admits, "I have been a trouble-maker." Even his acceptance speeches for major awards are so offensive, audience walks out, and elderly lady attacks him with her umbrella getting on bus. Bernhard denounces hypocrisy, provokes scandal: "To shake people up, that's my real pleasure." Novels, written as monologue in digressive style, without paragraph indentations, show black humor, pessimism, fury at human cruelty. Typical format employs protagonist based on real-life model, an obsessed genius intent on perfection who's defeated by realization of absurdity of quest.

1983 Italo Calvino's funny, inventive, and original novel *Mr. Palomar* is published the year of his death. Philosophical book describes quest for fundamental truth. Preoccupied with the act of storytelling, 1979 novel *If on a Winter's Night a Traveler* is fiction about fictions. The writer and his reader are central characters. Theme is "process of creation, construction,

and consumption of The Book." Gore Vidal says that while other writers "look for the place where the spiders make their nests, Calvino has not only found this special place but learned how himself to make fantastic webs of prose to which all things adhere."

1984 Czech-born Milan Kundera publishes *The Unbearable Lightness of Being* during exile in France. Novel is set in Czechoslovakia after brief thaw of reform and optimism of Prague Spring, followed by crushing Soviet invasion of 1968. In novel, 2 couples express despair of life under totalitarian state, competing claims of flesh and spirit, and sense of life as weightless, due to insignificance of individual in world without meaning. Philosophical digressions interweave in existentialist works. References to music are

common, as are irony, humor, eroticism, and themes of exile and search for identity.

1984 Northern Ireland–born poet Seamus Heaney publishes *Station Island* collection. Poems treat—with great economy, concrete imagery, and musical language—the mythology, history, and complex politics of Ireland. Best-known Irish poet since W. B. Yeats embodies rural scene in fresh, clear, sensual word pictures. The 1995 Nobel Prize citation notes award is "for works of lyrical beauty and ethical depth, which exalt everyday miracles and the

living past." Heaney believes poet's task is to ensure survival of beauty, especially when threatened by tyrannical regimes.

1984 August Wilson's play on African-American life *Ma Rainey's Black Bottom* premieres in New York. Wilson's series of 10 plays portray blue-collar life in Pittsburgh and Chicago and feature music and speech of the streets (shown, blues singer Robert Johnson). At a cigar store in Pittsburgh frequented by Pullman porters, Wilson absorbs the cadences and slang of

their lingo: "I just loved to hang around those old guys—you got philosophy about life, what a man is, and what his duties, his responsibilities are." Range and depth unmatched in American drama; turns history of struggle into song of a people, what Wilson calls "both a wail and a whelp of joy."

New Journalism

New Journalism arises in the 1960s and '70s, adapting techniques of fiction (like literary style, personal voice, imagery, and humor) to nonfiction. Norman Mailer produces brilliant, semidocumentary accounts of politics (*Armies of the Night*, 1968); Capote brings a lush style and personal involvement to the investigation of a crime (*In Cold Blood*, 1966); and Tom Wolfe uses baroquely ornate descriptions and an exclamatory tone to capture the antics of pop hero Ken Kesey. Gripping dialogue, personality-infused commentary, and headlong 1st-person narration make these accounts as fun to read as a novel. Although Impressionistic and subjective, the style becomes increasingly popular. Hunter S. Thompson takes it to an extreme in his alcohol-permeated "gonzo journalism." Describes Richard Nixon as "a man with no soul, no inner convictions, with the integrity of a hyena and the style of a poison toad."

1988 American playwright Wendy Wasserstein's *The Heidi Chronicles* dramatizes, with poignant humor, plight of educated woman's conflicting ambitions, needs, and desires. Explores disenchantment of independent woman in male-dominated society. *The Sisters Rosensweig* (1992) is family dramedy in which 3 middle-aged sisters sort out questions of meaning in their lives. Typical heroine is single, sassy, and successful, seeking love but corroded by self-doubt and betrayed by conventions of society.

1985 Carlos Fuentes's *The Old Gringo* is fictionalized version of Ambrose Bierce's last days in Mexico. Fuentes examines Mexican soul through prism of Spanish, indigenous, and Mestizo cultures. Portrays greed, class warfare, and subversion of progress offered by revolution. Metaphorical exposés explore past and present, conscience and corruption of nation. Stream-of-consciousness technique in *The Death of Artemio Cruz* (1962) produces panoramic, multifaceted portrayal of life.

1987 In novel *Beloved,* Toni Morrison blends real struggles and surreal folklore to encompass magical in ordinary life. Her characters pursue path of self-awareness and cultural identity, contending with destructive racist, biological, and political forces. African-American author depicts life and legends of black people through shifting narrative techniques. Nobel Prize in 1993 honors Morrison, "who, in novels characterized by visionary force and poetic import, gives life to an essential aspect of American reality." Despite formidable obstacles her characters confront, "My project rises from delight," Morrison writes, "not disappointment."

1989 Richard Wilbur's *New and Collected Poems* wins Pulitzer Prize. American poet's carefully crafted, verbally dexterous poems employ diverse traditional forms and vary in tone from light to tragic. Explores how the real and apparent are interwoven, and the capacity of imagination to create reality. Love of nature is evident in fresh imagery of minute wonders of natural world. "Juggler" illustrates his delight in generating abstract idea from lovingly visualized particular: "When, in the air / The balls roll round, wheel on his wheeling hands, / Learning the ways of lightness, alter to spheres / Grazing his finger ends, / Cling to their courses there, / Swinging a small heaven about his ears."

1991 Brian Friel's tender play *Dancing at Lughnasa* opens on Broadway, showing Irish playwright's gift for lusty rural language and willingness to explore workings of human heart. In the play, a fictionalized memory of his 1930s childhood in Donegal, 5 Irish sisters find meaning for their lives at a pagan harvest fest. The women dance to celebrate life before it changes forever. Colorful characters, bittersweet humor, and layered narrative make Friel's plays emotionally resonant. Shown, Rosaleen Linehan and Alec McCowen in a London production of *Lughnasa*.

1991 South African novelist and short-story writer Nadine Gordimer gets Nobel Prize. Racial and political complexities of apartheid are her themes. Inequities of harsh oppression conveyed in precisely written tales through irony and psychological observation. *Burger's Daughter* (1979), best-known novel, is banned in her own land; tackles search for identity and need for commitment to humanitarian goals. In Nobel speech, Gordimer says, "Writing is always and at once an exploration of self and of the world; of individual and collective being."

1991 Irish writer William Trevor publishes 2 short novels as *Two Lives*. In 1972 collection of short stories, *Ballroom of Romance*, the title story is 1 of best-known. Portrays loneliness of middle-aged spinster, trapped by obligation to care for crippled father, whose only joy is going to local Saturday-night dances, where she chases dream of love, knowing she'll settle for much less. Novels and short stories set in rural Ireland show reduced life with low-key humor, poignantly but without sentimentality. Typically characters are outsiders, lonely, haunted by both past and present, thwarted in quests for fulfillment. Endurance is primary virtue, but minor moments of illumination occur.

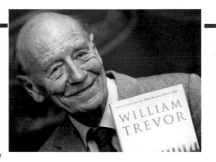

1993 Tom Stoppard's *Arcadia,* set in Derbyshire country estate, treats arcane subjects like English landscape design. Czech-born British dramatist's plot alternates between contemporary era and 1809; common element is difference between Classical and Romantic outlooks and chaos caused by sex. Other best plays are *Rosencrantz and Guildenstern Are Dead* and *Travesties*, full of verbal and scenic surprises and flights of inspired fancy where form and feeling merge. A sharp departure from realistic, "kitchen-sink" plays that dominate British theater when *Rosencrantz* (shown, Adrain Scarborough and Simon Russell Beale in a London production) 1st produced, Stoppard's thought-

provoking plays appeal more to head than heart. "It's wanting to know that makes us matter," character in *Arcadia* says. "Otherwise we're going out the way we came in."

1994 Peruvian writer Julio Ramón Ribeyro wins Juan Rulfo Prize, most coveted award in Latin American literature. Known for short stories, such as "The Jacarandas," published in anthology *The Word of the Mute*. Author explains title: "In the majority of my stories I give expression to those who are deprived of words in life, the outcasts, the forgotten, those condemned to an existence without communication or voice. I've restored to them their lost utterances and I've allowed them to assuage their yearnings, outbursts, and anguish."

1994 *Part II: Perestroika* of Tony Kushner's *Angels in America* wins Tony Award for Best Play. (*Part I: Millennium Approaches* won the Tony in 1993.) In 2-part, 7-hour epic play, ghosts and angels visit hero Prior Walter, a homosexual afflicted with AIDS in 1985. Play deals with tension between love for America and revulsion over its homophobia. Half black comedy, half tragedy is staged with deliberately artificial special effects. Dramatizes historical, personal, political, and universal themes of love, disease, tolerance, compassion, and death.

Memento mori

American Novelists, c. 2007

At the outset of a new century, the U.S. can boast of a host of fine writers producing novels of great literary power and achievement. A short list would include Cynthia Ozick, John Updike, Richard Ford, Jane Smiley, Richard Russo, Anne Tyler, Richard Price, Sue Miller, Russell Banks, Cormac McCarthy, E. L. Doctorow, and Ann Patchett. Two recently deceased authors who contributed classic novels to American literature are Thomas Flanagan (died 2002) and William Styron (died 2006).

Photo Credits

Index

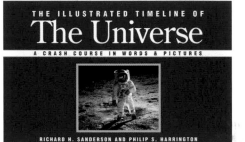